# Black, White and Carolina Blue

Dr. George T. Grigsby
Dr. Lucius Blanchard

Copyright © 2020

All Rights Reserved

ISBN: 978-1-80128-002-0

# Dedication

Thanks to our teachers at

Fuquay-Varina Consolidated High School

and

Ahoskie High School

for preparing us to reach

The University of North Carolina

and to

"all the people" in our "Carolina Family."

I am George Grigsby and proud to say:

I AM A TAR HEEL

I am Lucius Blanchard and proud to say:

I AM A TAR HEEL

# Preface

We have been promising this book for ten years. The first eight years the only thing we wrote was the title. Black White and Carolina Blue seemed to us and others like a pretty good name for some type of book but there was widespread doubt we would write the rest of it. We have now finished a story we can share. We want to tell it to our personal family members, our friends, our amazing scholarship students, and to all the people in the Carolina Family.

There is a long history here dating back to the university founding in 1789. There is a short story of our time there in the 1960's. If you, the reader, do not share part of that history, I hope you will also find the narrative interesting and entertaining. If you do, come spend a spring time day on the campus in Chapel Hill; see a fall football game against our biggest rivals; watch a Carolina/Duke basketball game in the Dean Dome-you will have to plan in your budget to purchase that ticket. Enjoy a lecture, a concert, or a Playmakers production. Enjoy our book and thanks for your support of the University of North Carolina.

# Contents

*Dedication* ............................................................................ *i*
*Preface* ................................................................................ *ii*
*Introduction* ........................................................................ *1*

*Chapter 1* ............................................................................ *4*
*Chapter 2* ............................................................................ *18*
*Chapter 3* ............................................................................ *29*
*Chapter 4* ............................................................................ *54*
*Chapter 5* ............................................................................ *65*
*Chapter 6* ............................................................................ *87*
*Chapter 7* ............................................................................ *96*
*Chapter 8* ............................................................................ *109*
*Chapter 9* ............................................................................ *125*
*Chapter 10* .......................................................................... *164*
*Chapter 11* .......................................................................... *187*
*Chapter 12* .......................................................................... *199*
*Chapter 13* .......................................................................... *212*
*Chapter 14* .......................................................................... *233*
*Chapter 15* .......................................................................... *247*
*Chapter 16* .......................................................................... *267*

*Epilog* ................................................................................ *280*

Page Left Blank Intentionally

# Introduction

I am by nature a solitary person. I am by nurture a reserved person. Fortunately for me, this has been balanced by having a few lifelong friendships. I have known Buzzy since we were both eight years old. He is not just a friend. He is a brother by choice rather than birth. Our relationship is as natural and unremarkable as many others. It has been constant for seventy years, so much so that our old school friends recognize us by our being together. At our fiftieth high school reunion, one of our classmates from the long past commented, "I recognize Buzzy, but not the other guy with him. He must be Luke."

This coming of age story is not about Buzzy. It is about an unlikely and unexpected friendship of sixty years. George Grigsby is not a person I could have played with as a child. He is not a person I could have met in grade school or accompanied to ball games or could have been at my senior prom. We could not have lived in the same neighborhood. Lincoln ended slavery but not segregation. I was born white and George was born colored. That was our designation in the south in the 1940s and 1950s. It is different now with different words and different attitudes. Young people of today, both white and African American, may know the recorded history of that era but not the pathos of that era. There are no more "White Only" or "Colored" signs on doors or drinking fountains to make it personal for them. There are other words and scenes here from that past time you will find inappropriate. They are offensive now and were then. To pretend it was not so is to deny how it really happened. There are also recorded here memories of unkind things from our impetuous youth. Things which we say if we could go back, we would have been different; we would not. We created who we are now.

George Grigsby and I were in college and medical school at the University of North Carolina at Chapel Hill in the 1960s. It was a time. I wish you could have been there. George did not want to write about it, so most of this is a narrative by Luke Blanchard. There is more about me than George; his preferred method of personal expression is canvas and paint rather than words. For years, I have been telling him that being one of the Black Pioneers coming to a previously segregated major university was his journey that should be remembered.

# BLACK WHITE AND CAROLINA BLUE

We are recording it now as an experience of two regular guys being friends for many years. It is not about conflicts-there were few. It is not about violent events-it is natural progress and changes in our lives. It is not even about a difficult friendship-it developed very naturally. It is about our history together and lives separate, and especially about our alma mater, The University of North Carolina at Chapel Hill, which shaped us and has always been a part of our lives.

George T. Grigsby and Luke Blanchard

# Chapter 1

The down east part of North Carolina is a flat coastal plain. In the middle of the state is the Piedmont and the capitol Raleigh. Farther west are the Allegheny Mountains. Streams and rivers wind through the flat plain, flowing slowly eastward in shallow channels that nourish the bottom farmland for the growth of cotton, tobacco and peanuts. The streams are the shade of light brown earth with soft muddy banks. The water has texture and thickness and moves so slowly it seems to be a part of the land itself rather than flowing through it. These streams fan out into the swamps and estuaries of the coast, then into flat warm sounds and through the inlets of the Outer Banks and make their way into the Atlantic Ocean.

This was originally a virgin pine forest. First, it was used to make tar and pitch to seal the old wooden ships. The workers were said to always have tar on the heels of their boots. Later the trees were harvested for their timber and to clear the fields for family farms. The rural counties are crisscrossed by two-lane farm roads. The paved main roads travel past towns and fields, and the dirt roads branch off sideways, going to the houses and trailers back in the woods on the few remaining farms where people still live. Here there are old houses once white or maybe painted but now fading to dark and brown by time and weather. They are surrounded by brown dirt yards and housing families also often brown. The tracks of the Norfolk Southern Railway go through this area. People and goods travel between the states up north and places like Atlanta, Florida and small southern towns. Other tracks head west from the farms to the cities and factories and tobacco mills in the Piedmont and to the North Carolina mountain towns and to states far beyond.

A community may develop where a highway and train tracks cross. Soon there is a general store selling grocery items and farm supplies to the people in the area. A small church is built where everyone can gather. Later there is a garage and gas station, and a few houses strung out along the highway on both sides of the crossing. If they grow and thrive, they will get a name that becomes their identity. It may be taken from a first resident family or the name of the church or sometimes an obscure name that has an unremembered meaning but might be an old Indian word. There will be a sign at the edge of town announcing the population, and its award as an outstanding community some years in the past. These towns are scattered across the American south. There is not much to distinguish one from another to a traveler passing through with no reason to stop. Ahoskie, North Carolina, a crossing town whose name is obscure, but the old people have heard tell it was an Indian name, is where my parents moved me when I was two years old, before I had a memory of anyplace else in the world.

The first place I called home was a small white frame house on Katherine Street. It was located a half block from the main street of Ahoskie. Across the road was a big house belonging to an elderly lady whom I seldom saw outside but who let me climb in her big front yard tree. Beside us was another family from whom we rented the little house.

A block away to the left of my front porch was the town water tower and the peanut shelling plant where my brother and I used to jump in the discarded peanut shells piled outside. To the right of my front porch was the house of a man I did not know but who always wore a bandana to hide his face because he had no nose. Beyond that was an intersection with Main Street that had a stop sign, a general store, the movie theater and an appliance store. The main street was ten blocks along with an intersection at each end with stop-lights where it joined the state highway. One block up from my corner was Railroad Street, the train depot and the tracks that ran through the middle of town. In the center of town adjacent to the train station was a vacant lot called "no man's land." If it had been larger or prettier or more historical, it might have been a town square, but since it was none of those things, it was just a dirt lot where cars could park, and people meet.

The depot station was an old wooden building with an elevated platform for the passengers to board or leave the trains and for moving cargo on and off the boxcars that carried supplies. The boxcars were painted with the names or initials of railroads from all over the country. They reminded boys in small towns that we were connected to distant places, even if we were not sure where they were or how far away they might be. The station building had two waiting areas with ticket windows, one outside and one inside, two drinking fountains, and two sets of bathrooms.

A large sign with Ahoskie written on it was placed on each end of the building notifying passengers at which town the train was stopping. The yard extended several blocks along each side of Railroad Street, where there were warehouses and feed stores and building supply centers that shipped on the trains. There was a siding track with boxcars ready for loading or just sitting empty, waiting to be called to travel to some other place.

Beyond the warehouses, the tracks went past homes, over small streets, under the overpass and over the trestles. Then they were away past fields and through forests until the next stop miles across the countryside or the next factory town or big city or even to distant destinations whose names or initials were painted on those box cars that went past the little train station with Ahoskie written on it in two places.

The school building for all white students was at the end of Main Street where it intersected with the state highway. All twelve grades were taught in the same building. The front schoolyard is large with many old trees and a tall white flag pole in the center. The main building has a center section with wings on both ends. Behind that are the gymnasium, the coal pile, the football field and other small buildings for shop class, music and home economics. This is where I was taught from the first grade to graduation, and I was with most of the same people and friends for the entire time. Along Main

Street were some of the old original houses that were always maintained in good condition. The town library, police station and volunteer fire department were all located inside the same building. There were two cafes, a movie theater, a pool hall, grocery stores, a drug store and malt shop, and small family-owned businesses that could still be successful.

Parallel to Main Street on both sides were streets with small neat houses, churches and the youth center. Heading out to the highway past the railroad depot and "no man's land," there were long low buildings for the tobacco auctions and at the end of the main street was the other intersection with the state highway where there were a farm equipment sales company and the local dairy.

The tobacco warehouses were empty for most of the year. They would open at harvest time when the auctions began. This was the end of months of work which started when the tobacco plants were first laid out in beds, nurtured through the summer, harvested and then hung in long tiers that were stacked to the ceiling in old wooden barns where it cured. Then it was ready for sale. The sweet smell of tobacco leaf spread from the warehouses to the surrounding neighborhoods and to Main Street. If the crop was good and the auction prices high, then mortgages were paid and new tractors and appliances were ordered, and new school clothes bought. After the auction the buildings were cleaned and the annual harvest dance was held in them. It was the brief autumn time of success, prosperity and celebration in our town.

After a few years on Katherine Street, my parents moved me to a bigger house close to the school. I got another brother and sister and met my best friend Buzzy, who lived a few blocks away. We became lifelong friends and his parents were a second family to me. Our house was on a large lot where I had my own trees to climb whenever I wanted. I got my dog named Playboy and he went everywhere with me. A girl named Bobbie lived a block behind me and I liked her a lot and often rode my bike by her house to see if she would notice me. There was another part of Ahoskie, east of Main Street, and across the railroad tracks as different from my world as another country. There were no paved streets or sidewalks. Ditches bordered the roads and were full of weeds and uncollected trash. The few stores were small and many of the houses neglected and vacant lots common. The nicest brick buildings were churches and the school for this neighborhood. This section was called colored town, as well as other names. All small southern towns had an area like this. We never had a reason to visit or to know anyone from there unless they came to work for us.

We had, at times, a colored housekeeper and cook and baby sitter. They used the back door of our house and we called them by their first names regardless of their age and we knew little about them once they were gone. My favorite was Naomi who was young and pretty and when she took care of me, showed me how to play jacks and sang songs I liked.

These were the boundaries of my youth in Ahoskie, North Carolina. They were both physical boundaries and the boundaries of tradition. The railroad crossing that became a small town was both safe and limiting. If you grew up here, you would never be far from someone who knew you and would take care of you. We were safe and protected without being aware of it because we did not know there was any other way to be. It is special to its residents, a brief stopover for travelers, and a home place to return to visit for those who left. It was true friendships that lasted. There were minor disputes that faded. There were major football rivalries. We had our schools and churches and farms and safe streets and residents that were genuinely friendly. I knew at a very young age I would have to leave Ahoskie as soon as possible and would never come back, but I did not yet know where I would go or what would happen to me.

I went through grade school and junior high and into high school without much notice. I was small and not athletic, and smart but not one of the top students. I was likable but not in a special way. Buzzy was always my best friend. He was tall and handsome and the most popular boy in our class. I had a few other close friends. We were Boy Scouts and Sunday school people and some of us Future Farmers of America and some destined for farms and trades and some of us on the college preparatory educational track.

The teachers favored the smarter students and the town kids over those who rode the bus in from the country. I was one of those favorites. They also favored the students whose parents were their friends. I was one of those. I was also fortunate to be there when the greatest generation was returning home. They came from winning a war to start building their families and their country. They were confident that they would make a society in which their children would have the opportunity to do better than they did. It was a boom of babies destined for great accomplishments. I was the firstborn son of a white middle-class family from a small southern town, and everyone expected me to be successful. One day in the ninth grade I discovered where my success would come from.

My class in the freshman year of high school had the usual day trip to our capitol Raleigh to learn about our state and it's history. Going up to Raleigh on a bus is about a three-hour trip. The Capitol is named after Sir Walter Raleigh. He was a member of the Elizabethan court who had ambitious dreams for his place in the new world. He sponsored expeditions to claim land in North Carolina for himself and his partners. Sir Walter never personally reached North America but sent several shiploads of colonists to settle the area, and they founded the famous Lost Colony on Roanoke Island on the outer banks of North Carolina. Unfortunately, Sir Walter's ambition and his land claims, like his colony, and eventually his head, would be lost.

Raleigh is also the location of North Carolina State University and is part of the research triangle along with Duke University in Durham and the University of North Carolina in Chapel Hill. Together these universities are known nationally for research, education and social progress, and some would say a breeding ground for radical ideas. It is a liberal island in a state that is very conservative in both east and west directions.

One of the stops on our school trip was to the state penitentiary, where we saw the prison yard and the cellblocks and the gas chamber. The inmates called to us as we walked through the facility. It was enough to persuade me that I did not want to end up a prisoner there. We visited Duke University, which was built in the class gothic style of English schools and was very impressive in its architecture and landscaping. It is like a private New England Ivy League school in the south and mostly attended by out of state students. Duke looked and felt out of place in the rural culture to which I was accustomed. I was sure I did not want to go there. We went to the University of North Carolina in Chapel Hill. It is a beautiful colonial-era campus with brick buildings surrounding upper and lower quads that are crossed by brick sidewalks and decorated with many small gardens with colorful flowers. It had its first class in 1795 and was the first public university in the United States. The main quad still has towering trees that had been planted there when the university was first built. The symbol of the university is the Old Well in front of South Building. It is where the original students drew out water and is now a drinking fountain. The Old East and Old West buildings are still original standing dormitories.

Sometimes the feeling that you belong somewhere arrives without knowing exactly why, but it is immediate and reassuring. It fits the place you were looking for without know what it would be. I knew this was the place to which I should go. There were still three years of high school left, and lots of things to be done and goals accomplished along the way to make it happen. The most important thing is that now I knew where I would go when I left Ahoskie. I finished high school without any problems. I was with the same group of boys and girls most of the time. A few moved away or new ones came for various reasons, and a few came to be at a small country school where there was no push for racial integration which was happening in some of the larger schools in the state. We went from being Boy Scouts to Explorer Scouts.

Some of my classmates became sweethearts and lovers and married, but it did not happen to me. I played several instruments in the school band, all badly. The basketball team at the University of North Carolina won a national championship in 1957 in one of the greatest games ever played and I liked them even more. Buzzy and I remained best friends all the way through school.

As the senior year approached, it was time to decide where we would go after graduation. I was still determined to go to UNC and major in English and writing. My grades were good but not in the top tier, so my teachers and advisors thought I should look elsewhere since there was the possibility I might not be accepted at Carolina. There was also the problem of paying for college. My family had enough money to pay for normal everyday expenses, but there were no extra funds to pay for a college education. Despite all these obstacles, I knew that Carolina was where I should be and was sure that I would get there, so it was the only school to which I applied for admission and scholarships and loans.

In our senior year we took the SAT test as part of our preparation for applying to colleges. The score on this test was very important in determining where a student would be accepted. My memory of taking the test is quite indistinct but it became very important. I got the highest SAT scores that anyone in my high school had ever achieved; of course, I and everyone in Ahoskie High School knew that was just lucky guessing on a lucky day for me.

After I sent my application to UNC, I went for a personal interview with the admission committee members. It was held in South Building, where I had first visited the campus three years earlier. They reviewed my file and said that my class grades were good, but my test scores were exceptional, and they thought I would do well at Carolina. I had been accepted there and given enough scholarship and student loan assistance to cover the cost of my four-year education. This is what I had been hoping for, and in youthful expectation, knew was going to happen without any thought otherwise. I was going to UNC. Some days you just get lucky.

# Chapter 2

It had been only a few years since the Revolutionary War was won. George Washington had been elected to his first term as president of an association of states and commonwealths that had not yet decided to become a united nation. There were 390,000 people living in North Carolina, of which 100,000 were enslaved persons of color. Most freemen and slaves lived and worked on isolated family farms in the rural areas and many were uneducated.

In the year 1789, the new state governors decided it was necessary to establish an institution of higher learning that would be of the people and for the people of North Carolina and supported by the state. In 1795 Hinton James walked for two days from his home in Hanover County to Chapel Hill and became the only student at the University of North Carolina, the first public university in the United States to open its doors.

One Hundred and sixty-five years later, in the autumn of 1960, I rode in my family car from Ahoskie to Chapel Hill, a distance of about three hours. I was the oldest child and the first to leave home, so my parents, brothers and sister accompanied me on the trip to see where I was going and say their farewells. In retrospect, I wonder if they understood that for me, this was a separation from my childhood home forever and that I would return for visits but never live there again. It was a separation both in the distance and challenges, and with opportunities that would not have existed in my home town. We rode around the campus and down the main street, Franklin Street, and I showed them all the things I had learned from my study about Chapel Hill. Then it was time for them to leave for the return drive home.

They dropped me off in the center of campus by the Old Well with my cardboard suitcase of clothes and personal items and with three hundred dollars that had been given to me by my grandmother as a high school graduation present. Now I was a student, one of about 2000 freshmen at Carolina, arriving for orientation week. I had thought about this many times, and I was now where I had always planned to be. I went to South Building, the main office building of the university. I got my dormitory assignment and basic information about where things were located and the schedule for orientation sessions.

I was placed in Alexander Dormitory, an all-male dorm in a quad a block from the central campus. At this time UNC was attended almost entirely by men except for some women in the health sciences, and some liberal arts and graduate students. There was a separate dorm for women since the concept of co-ed living was not accepted.

I had a small room, #106, on the first floor that I shared with a roommate named Lewis from Wake Forest who was also assigned there. There were about twenty-five similar rooms on our floor and a central bathroom for all to use. Outside the dorm were tennis courts and behind the building was the Chapel Hill Cemetery. This was a wooded area with trees and grave sites going back hundreds of years.

I am a solitary person by nature and this was to become, for me, a place I would visit for refuge, reading and contemplation in the presence of people now in their own permanent place of refuge and peace. Woollen Gym was nearby for basketball and all the sports activities. Kenan Memorial Stadium, where football was played in the fall, was behind that. Across the street was the baseball field. Despite my introverted nature and desire for privacy at times, I adapted well to life at UNC and in the dormitory.

Although Lewis was quite extroverted and gregarious, he respected my different temperament and we got on well. I quickly made a few friends in Alexander that shared common interests, and we went through orientation week together. Tom lived across the hall and was a recreation major and loved sports. I bought a wooden tennis racket for six dollars and some athletic shoes and played tennis with him.

I thought I might become more athletic and got gym shorts and shirts to go with my tennis shoes and a storage locker at Wollen gym where I could exercise and run in my free time. John lived several rooms down the hall and was from Raleigh and, like me, was planning to major in English. Michael, on the other end of the hall, was Jewish and from New York and was in premed.

Teddy was funny and friends with everyone, and only on rare occasions obnoxious. I was reserved but enjoyed making this group of new friends and getting to know each other in our communal living situation. During orientation week we had testing to determine our strengths and weaknesses. I was ranked advanced in English, average in the sciences, and very low in foreign language skills.

In high school I took courses in Latin but remembered little of it and found out that dead languages were not very useful in college. The foreign language requirement at UNC would become a source of continuing frustration for my academic adviser and me throughout much of my time there. He once referred to me as a foreign language academic coward after I first dropped German, and the next semester dropped French after a few weeks of classes to avoid any low grades in those subjects.

English was my favorite subject and easy for me. I was frequently at the public library in Ahoskie reading or checking out books on almost any subject. I read history and science and fiction and the great authors and classics. I regularly accumulated overdue book return fines at the rate of five cents a day, which I paid out of the money from my paper route earnings. The friendly librarian would usually reduce them if they got over 50 cents. I placed average in the sciences and planned to take the minimum number of those required classes to satisfy the graduation requirements. I spent time walking around the campus and looking at the old buildings, visiting Wilson library and the student center and arboretum, and some of the small stores along Franklin street. Since classes had not begun and the upperclassmen had not returned to school, the areas were only lightly frequented. I had beautiful fall days being in the main campus areas of Polk Place and McKorkle Place among trees that had been planted over a hundred years before. The symmetrical brick walkways across the quads had been worn smooth by the passage of thousands of students. The trees and flowers in the small gardens were putting on their autumn show. It was as good as I had expected.

After orientation week, all the students returned and we were officially freshmen. The dorm rooms were full and we started our classes. We met the teachers and professors who would instruct us that semester. We had not yet declared our majors, and since we were at the 101 level, the classes were large and many courses taught by grad students. I was fortunate to get an English teacher who appreciated my essay writing and encouraged me to continue it. My attempt at German was unsuccessful and the course was taught by a large intimidating woman whom I thought could have been an instructor in a German youth camp, so I dropped that course in a few weeks.

This was also fraternity and sorority rush week at Carolina. The fraternities worked hard in promoting the social life at UNC. A few of my new dorm friends and I signed up for rush week, but since I was on a financial need scholarship, I could not join a fraternity. We went to some of the Greek houses and pretended we were interested and also tried to be irritating enough to see who got the most black balls after the first visit. I actually got accepted at one fraternity but knew it would not work for me, so I declined.

Since I was on a need scholarship, they also assigned me a job to earn some extra income. I went to work at Lenoir Cafeteria, the main dining hall for the university. My job was mainly bussing tables, and occasionally I would be assigned as a cook for the breakfast shift. We were paid in script that was redeemable for food. Breakfast was twenty cents and lunch or dinner fifty cents for which we were given vouchers in a coupon book each month.

I also visited the Rathskeller in a basement off Franklin Street. It was a German restaurant and a popular place for the students since it served beer and barbecue and sandwiches. I had never had any alcohol and never developed a taste for beer, but it was a fun place to visit with friends once in a while. The Porthole was another popular eating place and was known for its excellent southern style biscuits. Orientation week, rush week, and the excitement of a new adventure slowly became a routine of classes, studying and working, and enjoying the ambiance of university life. There were new people, new ideas, and long late-night discussions in the dorm rooms or study halls or library on subjects that would have never been considered in my home or high school.

We talked about how one should live and is there any meaning in death. We discussed religion and Russia and communism and money and race relations, and would any of us date or marry outside our race or faith, and should you ever draw to an inside straight if the pot was big enough. There was never a consensus, even on drawing to the straight.

"What it was, was football" said a famous Tar Heel. In the 1960s, basketball had not yet reached its present position as the predominant sport at UNC, and students and alumni still remembered Charlie "Choo Choo" Justice. Saturday afternoon football, especially between the teams along Tobacco Road were the major events in the fall and a big celebration on campus. There were parades, parties, pep rallies and bonfires for the biggest games against N.C. State and especially against Duke, our biggest sports rival. In those days, the students could get tickets to all the games as part of their school fees, and the seating section for them was on the home side in midfield. Alcohol was permitted in the stadium, and underage students became the most ardent fans who would drink in celebration of a win or in the consolation of a loss.

In Alexander dorm we had keg parties and drinking contests before and after the home games. For the most part, I was an observer rather than an active participant, but still felt all the excitement of a true Tar Heel fan when college sports were for the love and glory of the contest and not the collegiate cash cow they have become in recent times. Charlie still stands in stature outside Kenan Stadium but seems out of place and time in the world of big money collegiate sports. But somethings never change and the words of "Hark the Sound of Tar Heel Voices" still fill the stadium and "Go To Hell, Duke." rings out when the Blue Devils come to town.

The fall term passed into the spring term, and I did well in all my classes except for my foreign language requirement. I enrolled and soon dropped a class in French. I became interested in campus activities and developed more friendships. I declared my English major and spent time in Bingham Hall, where most of the classes of that department were held and got to know some of the teachers well. The autumn season changed into winter, and the campus was sometimes decorated with snow that lay a few inches on the ground and the bare trees, and then it became spring, which is the most beautiful time in Chapel Hill.

The resurgence of the green canopy over the campus lawns, the bright flowers that line the brick walks, the trees that show off their Dogwood and Magnolia colors, and the brightest Carolina Blue sky that ever existed are why Chapel Hill is called the southern part of Heaven.

I visited Ahoskie a few times over the holidays. When summer came, I went to our family cottage at Kitty Hawk on the outer banks and spent time surfing and fishing and crabbing. My friend Buzzy went to college for a short time, then moved back home and took over his father's tile and carpet business and married his only high school sweetheart. It would last forever. As the hot summer beach days began to grow shorter, I became eager to return to school. I was going to be a sophomore at UNC.

# Chapter 3

I was born in Richmond, Virginia, in 1941 and named George Talmadge Grigsby, Jr. I grew up in Holly Springs in southern Wake County in North Carolina. The population then was slightly more than five hundred people and was where my maternal grandmother lived. Before moving to North Carolina, I lived with my parents in Lawrenceville, Virginia, where my father, George T. Grigsby, Sr., headed the trade school at Saint Paul's Institute.

Holly Springs is between the towns of Fuquay Springs and Apex. These towns are mainly farm communities where tobacco and cotton were the main crops. There were multiple tobacco warehouses where cured tobacco was auctioned. Sometimes my father would take me to the warehouses when our tobacco was being sold.

The home I lived in was two stories high. It had originally been built as a two-room farmhouse in the late 1800s, and in the early 1900s, an expansion and upper floor were added. It was one of the few houses in Holly Springs to have indoor plumbing and some central heating, especially in a black-owned dwelling. The rural streets were not always named and were noted by nearby landmarks, such as the brick church, or a blue house or the large old magnolia tree that everyone knew and admired. The largest house and one of the most historical places in Holly Springs was the Mims mansion. During the civil war, this house had been spared destruction by Sherman's army. The story is that the Yankees who stayed there reached an agreement with the owners that the house would not be destroyed if the owners were cordial with the occupying troops. My mother's friend, Ed Mims, was a descendant of the original owners and would show us through the house when he made major changes to it.

In the black section of town, the streets were not paved and sometimes became muddy when it rained. Sidewalks did not exist. White Holly Springs had paving and streetlights. I asked my father why this was so since we all paid taxes. He suggested I write to the town mayor and pose this question. Maybe my question encouraged my father in his decision to run for town commissioner. He worked hard getting blacks to register, and on the voting day, he offered free rides to those who had no transportation. Since Holly Springs had a significant black population, my father felt he had a good chance of winning one of the commissioner positions. My paternal grandfather, who had moved from South Carolina to Holly Springs, voted for his first time ever. My father did not win that year but ran the following year again and was elected then. I never received a reply from the mayor.

Shopping in Holly Springs was limited, and most businesses were owned by white residents. There was Ernie Brewer's grocery store, several gas stations, a hardware store, and a drug store. The drug store was where we received our school immunizations. We stood in line and waited our turn to receive an injection from a white nurse. There could be apprehension and crying but also maybe a Baby Ruth candy bar afterward.

There were a few black-owned businesses in the area, usually open in the evening and on weekends. One was a convenience store and pool hall owned by Green Prince. It was close to my house and the two black churches in our neighborhood, the Baptist Church and the Christian Church. There were some small black-owned cottage industries, mostly frequented by black customers, where food dishes such as chicken and pork and barbecue were available. Many of these places also sold bootleg whiskey-white lightning-which was illegal in our county. This attracted all types of people. In the evening whenever we saw a white man getting out of his car in the black part of town, we knew he was there to purchase alcohol. These places were generally tolerated, but occasionally there were raids to shut them down for a short while.

In 1954 my father opened his own store, the Packhouse. This was the typical country store where people could shop, gather to talk and share stories, and have a community center. There were games to play and a jukebox and a dance floor. I worked there in the summer. Sometimes I also worked with the tenants on our family farm where I had to pick cotton and pull tobacco, and I was usually the slowest field hand.

Working in the Packhouse was better. My father built this store, as well as some apartment houses, with concrete blocks that he poured himself. I sometimes helped with this also. My other job was on Saturday mornings when I delivered the Journal and Guide. This was a weekly black newspaper based in Norfolk, Virginia. The other black newspapers with which I competed were the Carolinian, which was based in Raleigh and had more local news, and the Afro, which was based in Baltimore, Maryland. I am sure I was selling the Journal and Guide because my father had gone to college in Hampton, Virginia. I had ten to twelve customers who were loyal. They were usually older black women. The newspaper sold for fifteen cents. I learned to extend credit when they did not have the money and would try to collect for this the following week.

On occasion, the customers pretended not to remember this, and I was not good at confronting them about collecting the outstanding debt. Except for the white paperboy, Jimmy Wright, a nephew of Ed Mims who delivered the daily News and Observer, there were no other paperboys. Many years later, Jimmy told me that my family was the only one who ever gave him a Christmas present for delivering the paper.

Wake County schools at this time were all segregated. In Holly Springs there was no operating school for white students. At one time there had been a brick schoolhouse near the railroad tracks that went through town, but that was now closed, and the students moved to a school in a neighboring city. I could walk to my first school from my house. On the street, it would take ten minutes, and if I took a shortcut on a footpath, it was five minutes. The school was a large frame building with four classrooms and an auditorium. Students from the first to the seventh grade were all in this building. There was no indoor plumbing. Toilets and a hand well pump were outside the building. The heat was provided from potbelly stoves in each classroom. There was no cafeteria, so students brought their lunches or went home to eat. Most of our teachers commuted from Raleigh each day, but the principal, Mr. W.E. Hunt, lived across from me during the week but returned to Raleigh on the weekends. I was a favorite of all the teachers and received much help from them.

From grades eight through twelve, I went to school at Fuquay Consolidated High School, a five-mile bus ride from Holly Springs. My father was a teacher there, and my mother also did some substitute teaching in the school. I learned that as a substitute, she was paid twenty dollars a day, which seems like a lot of money to me. There were about 30 students in my class. I was aware that this county school did not measure up to the city schools, which had a wider range of studies, resources, and activities. We had books that were marked and had missing pages since they had previously been used in white schools. There were no laboratory facilities, although the textbooks indicated that accompanying labs should be done to complete the subject matter. My science teachers would attempt to demonstrate such recommended labs since each class member could not be a participant. My parents never expressed these concerns, and my high school teachers were always encouraging.

I grew up in a very supportive environment. I am an only child but was part of a family of parents and grandparents and friends and teachers. My grandmother Alberta Stinson made sure I was a regular participant at church services and Sunday school at the Holly Springs First Baptist Church, which was prominent in our local community since it was established in 1866, one year after the end of the Civil War. I was exposed to a diverse environment. My mother was born in New York City and sometimes took me there in the summer to see her friends and for shopping and sightseeing.

There I could go to the movie theaters, and Broadway shows and not have to sit in the segregated balcony section as was still required in most of North Carolina theaters, and which my parents encouraged me to avoid. I was fortunate at a young age to have seen both these situations, and I knew there were opportunities available for me and that I would find them.

My parents, both college graduates, expected me to attend college. This was a fore-drawn conclusion. My paternal grandfather, Fred Grigsby, was a first-generation free black after the Thirteenth Amendment. He knew the importance of education and made sure that all of his eleven children attended and graduated from college.

My father, George T. Grigsby, Sr., graduated from Hampton Institute (HBCU now Hampton University) in Hampton, Virginia. My mother, Gladys Stinson Grigsby, graduated from Shaw University, a Baptist school in Raleigh, North Carolina, and received financial assistance from another Baptist school, Wake Forest College.

It was probably at the end of my freshman year in high school that my mother began to talk about what colleges I should consider. I was the top student in my class, and multiple options were possible. Leroy Burton's parents were both college graduates and friends of my family. Leroy was also planning to be a physician, so my mother thought we might attend the same college. It was decided we should both apply to Howard University in Washington, DC, and Hampton in Hampton, Virginia. My teacher also suggested his alma mater, Union College in Schenectady, New York, which had a good science department. I also began to look at the University of North Carolina in Chapel Hill. I was aware that no blacks had yet graduated from their undergraduate program, although some had been admitted there in the class of 1955; John Brandon, LeRoy Frazier, and Ralph Frazier, who all came from Durham, North Carolina. There had been four black men admitted to the Carolina Law School in 1951 and one to the medical school in 1961.

Without a doubt, Carolina was a first-rate university and had a medical school. I only knew one person who had graduated from UNC. A family friend, Ed Mims, had earned a degree in music and enthusiastically endorsed my application to Carolina. Financially Carolina was a better deal than the other schools under consideration, and it was only thirty miles from Holly Springs. Some of my friends worked there in Memorial Hospital and commuted daily, so I would know some people there and could get rides back and forth when needed. Carolina decals on car back windows were very commonplace in the area. I had always thought that if I saw a black person driving a car with this Carolina decal, the car was probably bought used, and the decal had not yet been removed.

Also, with Carolina being only thirty miles from home, it could become a sensitive issue if, for some reason, I had to leave school. It was rumored that the school superintendents, all of whom were white, threatened to fire any black principal who encouraged black students to attend white colleges. So I did feel some pressure in making Carolina my first choice.

I was very excited and a bit anxious when I learned I had been accepted at UNC. My acceptance was a thick envelope, which I felt was a good sign before I opened it. A rejection letter would have been only one page. I began to wonder if Carolina knew that I am black. Had that made any difference? What was going to happen when I got there? My high school principal did not lose his job.

The day my parents drove me to Chapel Hill, I was in an anticipatory mode. My father had difficulty with the correct spelling of Chapel Hill for a long time. He had grown up in Chappells, South Carolina. It was many years later that my mother told me how sad my father was to leave me sitting on a bench in front of the Grimes Hall dormitory. After getting settled in my room, I went to dinner at Lenoir Hall cafeteria, which was close to the dorm, and afterward said goodbye to my family as they left for the drive back to Holly Springs. I have reassuring memories of the cafeteria food servers who were older black women. When they saw me in line, they gave me a warm smile- a smile that said we are glad to see you and will take good care of you. During my eight years at UNC, they remained staunch supporters of all black students.

Often, they invited us to their churches and their own family events. It was a little family away from our families back home. It would take a while, but I could already tell that I had made the right choice and that UNC would become an important part of the rest of my life.

During orientation I learned campus landmarks. These included the Old Well, Wilson Library, Morehead Planetarium, and Silent Sam. We were told about tunnels beneath the campus grounds which connected all the buildings. There was one building that contained a very large computer. This was one of the few buildings which were air-conditioned since the computer required proper cooling to function. In my freshman year, I placed in honors classes in French and math. Afterward, I realized that being in a regular course would have been much easier. I also took some advanced

French and Spanish courses. I worked part-time in the language lab, where I provided tapes for students studying foreign languages. Luke remembers me from a Spanish class taught by Dr. Meadows and from meeting me when he came to the language lab, but I do not remember him from those encounters.

During undergraduate school, I remember I met a few students who dropped out of courses and were never seen again. Difficult required courses seemed to be a way of decreasing the number of premed students. There were rumors of suicides by ingesting cyanide or jumping from upper floors of classroom buildings. As an upperclassman, I met more students who were premed and pre-dental. Occasionally we would study together before the big exams. The fraternity students had files of old exams which were good to review before we took the tests, especially if the same professor was still teaching the course.

Since labs were taught by graduate students, they were a bit more relaxed, although spending long afternoons in the basement of the chemistry building during spring weather could be depressing. When we were divided into teams for work assignments, it was usually in alphabetical order. I don't remember anyone changing teams because I was placed with them, but I did wonder if team members had not been assigned would I have been chosen by anyone. In one biology lab we had to examine blood specimens, including our own. I reviewed my blood sample and saw red blood sickle cells. This is a sign of a dangerous blood disease that frequently appears in African Americans. After a few minutes of anxiety my lab partner told me it was not really my blood, but a teaching slide depicting sickle cell anemia.

During the eight years I attended the University of North Carolina, I was the only black student in my class. If I had wanted to cut classes, it would not have gone unnoticed. Being only thirty minutes from Holly Springs, it was not uncommon for me to call home on Sunday morning and tell my parents that I was bringing schoolmates for breakfast. My parents and schoolmates seemed to enjoy these gatherings. Occasionally on my visits to Holly Springs, I would be asked when I planned to graduate. The question was asked because it was not commonly understood how long it took to get a medical degree, and some people thought I was never going to finish school there.

Except for my last year in undergraduate school, when I lived in an off-campus house, I lived in Grimes dormitory. Grimes was located in the lower quad of dorms. It was usually where the law students resided since the law school was close and an easy walk away. The law school has since been moved across campus into a newer building. I think that all single black male students living on campus, whether undergraduate or graduate, were assigned to live in Grimes dormitory.

My roommate was Baalam Thalphonsa Elliot. He preferred to be called Thal. Thal and David Mozart Dansby had entered the Carolina class one year earlier and had successfully completed the freshman year. Thal was premed, and David was prelaw. There were other black students in Grimes who were in law school.

Both Thal and David were interested in my background; my high school, parents, and hometown. Being from a larger city, Greensboro, David had attended a much bigger high school. I think he was concerned about how a country boy was going to cope with Carolina. Although I had an undergraduate adviser, Thal was able to point me in a more precise direction when I chose my premed courses. In choosing my freshmen first-semester courses, Thal and David advised me which professors I should avoid since they felt they might not be teacher-friendly toward black students.

This could end up as a failed course. I did have one of these teachers in a math course. On the first exam, I made a perfect score. I'm not really sure what happened, but Thal and David were surprised and happy about it. Maybe after having previously successful black students, the instructor had adjusted his teaching attitude toward black students.

First semester freshmen had to take a swimming class as part of the physical education program. A requirement for graduation was the ability to swim. I was anxious about not being a confident swimmer and had never been in a swimming pool with white people before. There was no swimming pool in Holly Springs. In Raleigh, the swimming facilities were segregated; Pullen Park for whites and Chavis Park for blacks. I had been to Jones Beach in New York, which was integrated but did not feel that this counted very much. We all gathered around the indoor pool in Woollen Gym, and the instructor yelled, "everybody in the pool" that was it. It seemed no problem for any of us as we all stood wet and shivering in the cold water.

David was more revolutionary than I was, and he felt I should have been more passionate whenever race became an issue. That was not part of my nature, but I knew he always had my best interest in heart when he brought these things up to me. Thal, David, and I were very active in some campus activities where we tried to make a difference in the university, and its attitudes. Ann Queen, who was the head of the Y on campus, was influential in helping make some of them successful.

Our classes were timed so that we had ten minutes to reach the next class. This sometimes required a brisk walk if the next class was in a building some distance away. The chemistry building, Venable Hall, was one of those buildings. In my haste to reach a chemistry class there, it was not uncommon for me to be bumped off the brick walkway onto the manicured grassy lawn. I remember it being especially true on this particular walkway and occurring with more frequency and becoming intentional and with more ferocity.

I decided that I must evaluate this situation and confront the aggressor. When it did occur next, I stopped and looked defiantly at the person. He was taller than I, but I persisted. He laughed and acknowledged that he was in my chemistry class and admitted to being the person who had been doing this all along. I was relieved, and Carroll Gray and I ultimately became good friends. He did his medical internship and residency at George Washington University, where I also trained. One of the highlights of my time at UNC was when Dr. Martin Luther King visited the campus as a guest lecturer. I was invited to a welcoming dinner with him, which occurred before the lecture.

We did not have the opportunity to discuss any issues there, but I found him to be an impressive and receptive person and was proud to meet him and support the ideals he represented. At this time, blacks were not allowed in the off-campus movie theaters on Franklin Street. With the exception of the Rathskeller, I don't recall being able to eat in any restaurant on Franklin Street. On Friday evening, free movies were shown on campus. All campus dining rooms and the Carolina Inn were open to blacks. On occasion, there would be awkward moments when I was invited to join my fellow students to see a movie or dine at a restaurant in town, and of course, I would have to decline. When they persisted, I would have to give the real reason.

I was warmly received at one place on Franklin Street. I attended the University Baptist Church near the campus. It was a diverse congregation, and I was welcomed there. I was also introduced to the church's Baptist Student Union (BSU), which was located on Rosemary Street, a short walk from the campus. We had weekly Sunday evening meetings, which included meals. Socially this was a friendly group of Carolina students with various interests, which included nursing and premed.

During my freshman year, a number of students, Carolina faculty and Carolina associates, separated from the University Baptist Church to form the Olin T. Binkley Baptist Church. The minister was Dr. Robert Seymour. Attendants of this church included Carolina students and the Carolina basketball coach Dean Smith who was also a member here. He would frequently attend with some of the players from his team. I was invited to join this church and did become a member and remained a member of this church until I left Carolina.

I applied to UNC medical school and was invited for an interview as were many of my premed friends. My anxiety had reached a high level as it got closer to the day when med school admissions were to be announced. My undergraduate roommate Thal was now a first-year Carolina medical student. On the day before the admission announcement was made, he informed me that I had been accepted. How he knew this, I do not know. Of course, I really was not sure until I had the admission letter in hand, saying I had been given a place in the first-year medical class and a scholarship for four years. My class had sixty-five students, two of whom were female and one black. I found medical school much more competitive.

Not only were there students from UNC, but also from Davidson and Duke University and a few from out of state schools. Charles Graham was in medical school a year ahead of me. He had been a cheerleader at Carolina, and later moved to Topeka, Kansas where I also lived for awhile and he became a good friend. All of these people were very well qualified and eager to reach the top of the class rankings.

Single medical school students usually lived in Craige Dorm, which was newer and closer to the medical school and hospital. Craige was arranged in suites, with each unit having four rooms with two students each and a central bathroom. I first remember meeting Lucius Blanchard, who moved into the room next door to me. He was in the first year of medical school, and I was then starting into my third year. There was no cafeteria in Craige, but nearby Eringhaus dorm did have a cafeteria where we frequently ate. On special occasions we would visit the Carolina Inn cafeteria, which had more variety and good food presentations. If I wore my short white medical school jacket, I would sometimes be asked to carry their tray by other patrons of the Carolina Inn cafeteria.

I would point out one of the waitstaff who could help the patron who by then was very apologetic for mistaking me for one of the waiters. The first two years of medical school did not offer any contact with live patients. There was more science to be learned. Anatomy class was the most intense with classroom lectures and laboratory sessions in the cadaver room. The labs always had the smell of formaldehyde. A team of four students worked on each cadaver. Our cadaver was an older black male. Most of the cadavers used for the study were black. By the semester end, we had become intimately acquainted with our subject as we had dissected all the body systems except the brain.

Neuroanatomy was quite challenging. Again, we learned through lectures and laboratory sessions. During the labs, when speaking to me, the professor made comments which I found tantamount to racial taunting. I decided to be dismissive of his remarks but found that his class was not an optimal learning environment for me. My clinical rotations began the junior year. At this time, we were allowed to wear short white jackets and carry our stethoscope in a pocket or around our neck. We were assigned to see patients at the North Carolina Memorial Hospital Clinics and inpatient wards. NCMH was a referral hospital and received patients from all over North Carolina. These patients were difficult to diagnose and treat because the local referring physician might not have the resources, experience, or be willing to take the time required to look for the correct diagnosis.

At this time, I remember the hospital was racially segregated. Only occasionally did white patients refuse to allow me to take their history and do a physical exam. What initially did surprise me was when a black female patient refused to allow me to take her history and do the physical exam. The patient asked for a white doctor. A younger relative usually accompanied the patient and would explain that this black doctor was as good as a white doctor. That relative would apologize to me and explain that the patient had never been treated by a black physician. We also had rotations through a nearby prison where we did sigmoidoscopic exams. On one occasion, the prisoner I was getting ready to scope, saw me and said, "Talmadge, is that you?" He was a neighbor from Holly Springs.

I spent some time in Raleigh at Wake Memorial Hospital to do an internal medicine rotation and at Dorothy Dix mental hospital, where I had a psychiatric rotation. During my senior year, my father died of a pulmonary embolus while hospitalized at Wake Memorial Hospital. In my senior year, Luke and I went on a road trip to Washington and New York so I could do some interviews to decide where to go for my internship. I was offered a position in the internal medicine department at George Washington University Hospital and accepted it.

That is where I would go after graduation. At my medical school graduation ceremony, I had a number of friends and relatives attend. My uncle, Snow Flake Grigsby, was editor of the Postal Alliance and brought along his photographer to document the graduation. I think I was the only graduate that day, June 6, 1966, who had a personal, professional photographer. George Washington University Hospital (GWUH) is the main teaching hospital for GW Medical School. Two other students, Bernie Credle and Carroll Gray had graduated with me at Carolina and were also at this hospital. I was a straight medicine intern meaning most of my instruction would be done in that specialty. I was pleasantly surprised to find the Chief medical resident Dr. Hannibal Howell to be black. Since leaving high school in 1958, I had never had a black teacher or instructor. The medical students, house staff, and attending physicians were ethnically diverse, and females were well represented.

GWUH was the hospital for many government workers, which included members of Congress. These patients did not always embrace and would mildly protest being cared for by a team, which included interns, residents, and the attending physician. Often the most high-profile patients would be admitted under an assumed name to preserve their real identity. Toward the end of my straight medicine internship year, I was asked to stay at GW as a first-year medical resident. I ended up doing my first and second-year residency there before moving to Boston for a third year in internal medicine training. While a resident, I was pulled aside by a few interns who worked under me, and they told me that some of the interns had concerns that they would not be fairly graded. I asked why they had this concern. I was told that because they were Mormon, it was felt that my being black might influence me to grade them negatively. At this point, I was completely naive about the Mormon church and racism.

I was able to assure the interns that this would not be a factor in grading. I did have flashbacks of my neuroanatomy professor. Living in Washington was a big change from being in Chapel Hill and Holly Springs. Although it had some southern charm, it was not as friendly as NC. Here the local news was national news. Life was at a faster pace. Traffic could be daunting and travel circles challenging. A novice driver could go around the circle several times before being able to exit. I had a bright yellow Corvette, so I was very noticeable. Police also seemed to like to give traffic tickets to black sports car drivers. Since GWUH was right off of Washington Circle, I had to quickly learn how to navigate it.

Washington was designed by Pierre Charles L'Enfant, and when I became familiar with the plan, it was easy to navigate around the city. Getting in and out of Washington was made easy with nearby Union Station and National airport. I never had to search for a restaurant that served black people. They all did. There were lots of federal buildings and monuments, and on the Mall there were museums with free admission.

The White House was only a few blocks from GW. I managed several times to climb to the top of the Washington Monument. I learned to snow ski at Blue Knob Mountain in Pennsylvania, which was only a few hours away. Martin Luther King was assassinated in April 1968. There were several days of riots where I saw stores being broken into and appliances being stolen. Curfews were put in place. Essential workers received passes which allowed movement during the curfew. I have vivid memories of tanks on the deserted streets of our nation's capital. It was something surreal to me. Before leaving Washington, I was asked by some young internists who had been my attending physicians to consider joining their medical group after I finished my military obligation. I did like the idea but never followed through after my discharge from the Air Force.

# Chapter 4

It began in Greensboro, North Carolina, in Woolworths Department Store in February in 1960. Four customers had finished shopping and sat down at the store lunch counter. They each ordered a cup of coffee and waited patiently. They sat at the counter until closing time, and none of them were served. They were black, and the lunch counter was for whites only. They and some of their friends came back daily, and this non-violent sit-in began the end of segregation of Woolworth lunch counters.

Discrimination had been their policy in the southern department stores since their founding in 1878. Similar peaceful sit-ins, encouraged by Martin Luther King, spread thought out the southern region. The Howard Johnson restaurant in Durham had a demonstration by students from UNC and Duke and several black colleges in the area. In Chapel Hill the movie theaters were strictly for whites only. In 1961 students picketed the Varsity and Carolina movie theaters, which resulted first in admitting UNC students of color if they had a student ID card and later all black people.

## DR. GEORGE T. GRIGSBY AND DR. LUCIUS BLANCHARD

Undergraduate African American students were first allowed at UNC in 1955 when three of them were enrolled. In 1961 there were about 9000 students at Carolina, and less than 100 were African American. One of them was in my Spanish class, and his name was George Grigsby. He was the only undergraduate black student admitted to UNC in 1958. It was a little thing and a big thing; it was the first time I had been in an integrated class, and he would later become one of my best friends.

Most people of my parent's generation were prejudiced without knowing there was any other way to be. Small southern towns like Ahoskie were racist by long-held tradition and a strong belief of black inferiority. The state of North Carolina was strongly against any form of integration and had a Ku Klux Klan tradition that was still active in the 1950s and 1960s.

The most segregated places you could find were any barbershop on Saturday morning, any restaurant for an evening dinner, any church for a Sunday service, or any school on a weekday. The first three were by tradition and the last by separate but equal legislation.

The lessons a person learns from example when they are young are the most enduring and difficult to change. It is difficult because there is not just one event or fact or premise that can be attacked and refuted. The multiple accumulated layers of observed behaviors become normal. Growing up in my family and community and southern state, I had been taught no differently. Even then, I had the early recognition that this was not the only way and not the right way. I thought my parents and many of my friends could do better.

I decided that I could do better. Despite thinking this, it did not mean that I accepted the equality of blacks or the policy of equal rights or integration. My thoughts at that time, albeit formed in an incomplete way, were that black people were different, but we should be more respectful of them. There were still a lot of things to be learned, and Carolina was the place a lot of it would happen.

George Grigsby has been telling me for the past sixty years that he does not remember me from our first Spanish class together. I talked to him enough to learn a few things. He was from Holly Springs in North Carolina and worked in the university language lab, where I was supposed to go several times a week to listen to Spanish tapes. He was two classes ahead of me and was taking Spanish as an elective course, which I thought was unusual. My college adviser had forced me into the class as the easiest way to satisfy my lagging foreign language requirement. I was one of about thirty white students in the classroom, so there is no reason he would have any recollection of someone like me. That would come later.

I continued my education at Carolina and found summer jobs on campus so I could stay in Chapel Hill. I was still living in Alexander dorm and had a different roommate who was gay. We got along well and respected each other choices.

The protests against segregation became larger and more intense. Many of them were aimed at the stores along Franklin Street, such as the Colonial Drug Store and the College Cafe, which still refused to serve black customers. Most of these were peaceful pickets and marches in front of the stores. I participated in many of them but was not a dedicated activist and sometimes frequented the places we picketed when the protests were over. As the demonstrations became more violent, we were sometimes chased away by the police and the dogs, and occasionally a few of us were arrested. Some demonstrations took place in front of the post office and by Silent Sam, a statue of a confederate soldier that had been erected on the campus close to Franklin street. The statue was to honor the students and faculty of UNC who had served in the Confederate Army during the Civil War. The legend students knew about Silent Sam was that he would fire his rifle whenever a virgin walked by him. He had an empty ammunition pouch so he could never really fire a shot.

People driving into North Carolina were greeted with a highway billboard that said, "Welcome to North Carolina, you are in the Heart of Klan Country." There was an increase in KKK activities in our area, and several friends from the dorm and I heard about a large gathering that was happening in a rural area south of Chapel Hill. That night we went to a farm outside of a small town where many cars and trucks were parked along the road that led up to the site. In the middle of a cleared field there was a tall cross wrapped in white cloth, and next to it was an elevated stage. Surrounding the stage and cross were hundreds of people dressed in their white robes with white hoods over their heads. My friends and I stayed on the periphery since we did not know how we would be received by the klansmen. Several of them came by and talked to us, which made me uneasy, but they were polite and not threatening. They did not try to persuade us differently when we said we were not there to join the KKK, but just to watch. They gave us printed application forms to use for membership if we changed our minds.

There were several klansmen who spoke about the dangers of integration, racial mixing, and intermarriage. One of the interesting things was the difference in how they put the message. Some of them were articulate in their views and avoided racial hate words, while others were full of anger and venom. The last speaker climbed onto the platform.

He said, "my good friend here has been calling them Negros. I will tell you what they really are. And it starts with a little n and has two g-s in the middle. They are degenerates and dirty animals. The communists and the government want them in your schools. Soon they will be living in your neighborhood. And then those black bucks will be in your bed with your daughters! We are not going to let that happen, are we?" The mass of white robes and white hoods echoed their approval. A torch was handed up from the ground and waved in the air and then touched to the base of the cross.

Flames climbed up the pole and onto the cross members and up to the top of the cross, and the whole structure burned bright yellow and orange flames. Black smoke rose into the night sky, and the white robes cheered. We drove back to Chapel Hill with little conversation. We knew the recorded history of the Klan but had never experienced in person the power of the Klan. We came away with an entirely new frame of reference for how frightening it would have been for black people in the past when the Klan was still powerful and came with guns and ropes. We had been afraid, and we were just a group of curious white college boys.

Everyone in my age group remembers where they were on November 22, 1963. At 10:30 that Saturday morning, I was in Hanes Hall in an English class. It was a beautiful fall day, and we were getting ready for a homecoming parade and football game. Everything was normal until someone came running down the hall and opened the classroom door and yelled out that the president had been shot. We left the classroom quickly in various states of disbelief and shock and sadness. The parade and the party and the football game were canceled. To many people, this was the end of Camelot in Washington.

## DR. GEORGE T. GRIGSBY AND DR. LUCIUS BLANCHARD

President John Kennedy had been the speaker at UNC on our University Day on October 12, 1961. Many of us had attended his address in Kenan Stadium and felt a connection because of that. I was not a strong Kennedy supporter, but he and his wife, Jackie, were the new generation of politicians. In contrast to Dwight Eisenhower, they were younger and modern and glamorous, and we could relate to their generation more easily.

In many ways, we had our own Camelot in Chapel Hill. It was a university town that was liberal and progressive and safe. It was marked by definite geographic boundaries and surrounded by conservative rural communities where people thought differently than we did. When I told some people in Ahoskie where I was going to college, they said I was going there to become a communist and a nigger lover.

It was a story I had heard before; at my school, from men who owned white robes, and even from some of my relatives. We had our protected enclave in Chapel Hill with our professors and teachers as our mentors. Fellow students were our knight apprentices in training. We had celebrations and parades and parties. Sports were our tournaments. We felt the excitement of making things happen that we thought would change the entire country. If you were not fortunate enough to live in Chapel Hill in the 1960s, then you really missed something.

I did well in school and became an upperclassman and a very good English major. I had learned a lot of things at Carolina, and one thing I learned very quickly was that if you were talking to a girl, it was better to tell her you were premed instead of an English major. So, I started telling people I was premed even though I really was not.

There was no plan in my mind that I would ever really become a doctor. I had taken the basic required science classes and had decent but not great grades. After a while, I thought if I was telling people I was premed, I should take a few more premed classes. When I reached my early senior year, I had completed the bare minimum of required science classes to apply for medical school.

As an outstanding English major, I was in honors classes with a small number of select students. One of our writing teachers was Betty Smith, who was famous for her novel "A Tree Grows in Brooklyn." She was retired in Chapel Hill, and we would meet at her house, which was a block away from Franklin Street for our discussions. John Knowles was our writer in residence that year and had published a successful novel called "A Separate Peace." While I was in the program, I wrote some short stories that were rejected by several magazines, worked on a short novel, and had a great deal of fun with the teachers and fellow students in this open kind of learning format.

As I went into my senior year, I had to make some plans for the future. I applied for a position as a graduate student in fine arts at the University of North Carolina at Greensboro and was accepted into that program and offered a scholarship to go there. I had enough psychology classes to qualify for a second major in that department and was also in their honors program. I was offered a scholarship to do graduate work in psychology.

I also decided I would apply for medical school since I had taken the required basic courses and thought I might become interested in medicine as a profession, but considered it unlikely I would get accepted since my science grades were only average. When I went to my interview with the doctors on the admission committee, they said they had reviewed my application, and even though my science grades were not impressive, they were trying to add some diversity to the medical school class, and they wanted to admit some English majors. I was surprised to hear that I had been selected for admission to the School of Medicine and offered enough scholarships and school loans to cover the full cost of medical school. Thank you, UNC English department.

This was quite an unexpected outcome for me. I had never wanted to be a doctor and did not think I would be an especially good one. I did not have any long-felt desire to heal people and make them better, as my premed friends expressed. I doubted I would like to be around sick people as a full-time job.

Before I decided what to do, I discussed it with one of my psychology professors who said he thought I should go to medical school since there would be more opportunity for me in that direction. I also discussed it with my writing teachers, Betty Smith and Jack Knowles, who both advised without hesitation that I should go to medical school. I took that as a vote of confidence in my academic potential rather than a critique on my writing talent. I accepted the offer and was going to be a first-year medical student at the University of North Carolina and still a Tar Heel.

# Chapter 5

In the fall of 1964, I began my first year of medical school. I moved from Alexander Dorm to a suite of four rooms in Craige dormitory with a roommate named Joe. This dorm was closer to the hospital and medical school where I would be studying. After I settled into my room, I checked to see who else was living in the suite, and next door was George Grigsby.

I remembered George from my Spanish class, although he did not recall me. He was a third-year medical student. Our wing of Craige was primarily occupied by medical students. These were the people I would spend most of my time with over the next four years. My friend Earl lived across the road in Ehringhaus Dorm. He had graduated from Carolina and stayed there for dental school. Earl was someone with whom I had grown up. His father owned the local drug store in Ahoskie and sometimes let me read the comic books in his shop without buying them. Earl had wanted to be a dentist for as long as I had known him and did not apply to medical school with dentistry as a backup as did many medical school applicants.

I was one of the sixty-eight medical students starting that year. All of us were white, and sixty-three of us were male. It seemed diversity had not yet reached the UNC school of medicine. I was not destined to be an outstanding student. Many of my classmates had come from medical families and had known all their life they wanted to be a doctor. Some of them were there because they really wanted to help people. Others were there for the money and prestige or to please their parents. A few like me arrived because they wandered on a different path than they had anticipated.

The first two years of medical school were classes in basic sciences and were similar to our previous years of instruction. Courses were in anatomy, physiology, biochemistry, and related fields in biology. Our professors were leaders in the areas of their specialty, and we were the uneducated neophytes that might someday dream of replacing them. The concept of egalitarianism was not yet recognized, and we were expected to work long and difficult hours for little praise and to expect humiliation at times if we could not remember the Krebs Cycle or the clotting cascade or all the bones and muscles with their origins and insertions. The competition among students was fierce and relentless. A whole career might depend on getting high marks on exams, a good recommendation from a professor, and a good placement as an intern and resident. For some of us, the highest distinction of success was how many hours a day could be devoted to studying. Sadly, for several of my friends it would become a fatal journey.

I do not know why one of my fellow students jumped from the third floor of the medical school building or how my classmate and lab partner obtained the cyanide he took or what drove him to do it. If asked, I would have said they seemed to me like perfectly normal people, and I never saw anything like that coming. It frequently seems to be that way and makes it an even more surprising and sad event.

As I spent more time with George, I got to know him better. We had many things in common. We were both above average in intelligence but neither of us would be considered exceptional, especially among our classmates going into the medical field. Both of us were moderately ambitious, but neither of us was particularly driven. We liked some people moderately well but found many others to be tedious and irritating, especially the ones that were pretentious or as we used to say, not real people. George had planned to be a doctor since he was in high school Maybe that was because he came from a family of overachievers. Some of his relatives were accomplished painters, writers, media producers, and university executives. He also knew that as a young black man many good opportunities might not be available in other professions.

Holly Springs is a historically black town near Raleigh and was settled by many free people of color after the civil war. The oral history of the Grigsby family is that on his father's side, his great-grandmother was born from a slave and a white father.

After the end of the Civil War, his grandmother on his mother's side got some land in South Carolina, and later obtained some land in North Carolina, and moved to Holly Springs. His family was one of the most prominent and successful in the area and active in the local school, business, and politics. They owned several tracts of farmland and the local general store, the Packhouse, and some pieces of property in the city center. The longest street in Holly Springs is Grigsby Avenue. George was the valedictorian of his class and had his choice of many schools, including Hampton or

Shaw. These were the black universities from which his parents had graduated. He picked Carolina because it was close to Holly Springs and a place where he could get a good education, and possibly he could attend medical school there. There was some resistance from his teachers that their most outstanding African American graduate was going to a predominately segregated university, and George wondered if his race would be a factor, but this never presented any problem. He was accepted at UNC and placed in some of the honors classes.

George and I became good friends and ate together frequently. Sometimes Earl would join us. We attended movies and the occasional sporting event or campus activity, but George was not as interested in our college events or sports as I was. He was friends with Dean Smith, our basketball coach, and the one who was responsible for breaking the color barrier in the athletic program at UNC. George did not have many close black friends, but there was not much opportunity for that in Chapel Hill at that time. George had the ability to be comfortable with people of all races and to make them comfortable around him. We had a relationship that would not have been possible in either of our home towns. It was a skill that served him well at Carolina in a time when the acceptance of racial equality was not yet commonplace. I went with him to Holly Springs to visit his home place and his family's general store where I met his mother. She was also a teacher. When his father was in the hospital in Raleigh, I went with him to visit his dad before surgery. His father died a few days later from complications of the operation, and I was glad I had a chance to meet him.

My parents were not as understanding. We had a family beach house at Kitty Hawk, North Carolina. I wanted to invite George to come there with me for a weekend. However, my parents said that it would not be allowed. I had taken many of my friends to the beach before and when I asked why, I was told it was because we could not have colored people there. I was both angry and disappointed, but knew at this juncture nothing I could do would change what fifty years of history had done to make them the people they were now. The only real contact I had with patients in my first year of medical school was the anatomy class, and they were already dead. This was in a large room with dozens of embalmed cadavers laid out on plastic tables. We assumed that when they died of their illness, they either were unclaimed or had donated their body to the medical school. Memorial Hospital was the teaching hospital at the University of North Carolina and the public hospital for the state, and the place where the uninsured or unwanted or severely ill patient would evenly be received and possibly die. A team of three other classmates and I were assigned a body to dissect and study.

Week by week and month by month, we would open up different areas to examine the organ systems. Students on my team were fortunate in the body we were given. He was thin and well preserved and easy to work on. Some other teams had obese subjects, which required a lot of extra work to do an adequate exploration, and one of the adjacent teams had a cadaver filled with a fungus growing inside it, which had destroyed much of his brain and other organs.

Our professors were careful to instruct us on the importance of respect and dignity for the cadavers we were dissecting, but it was not always honored. First-year medical students getting their initial close experience to mortality in daily exposure to an embalmed subject will eventually find gallows humor. The nurses who had a cadaver in the same work area came into class one day and found their male body wearing a condom. No one knew how it got there or why he would need it. In my second year of medical school and Georges's final year, we took a trip together. I was accompanying him to see some of the hospitals where he was applying for his internship and residency. It would be fun, two people, one who happened to be black and one white who had become good friends going on a road trip together.

For me, it was a new experience because even though I had a close African American friend, we did still function in an almost totally white society. I had never been exposed to the black community, not even in that part of Ahoskie, where it existed in a completely segregated area.

It may seem strange to people now living in such a racially polarized society, but in that era of the mid-1960s, there was tension over the integration movement but also more civility and communication between people of a different color. At that time both peaceful and violent protests were initially limited to areas like Chapel Hill and Birmingham and Selma, but the daily lives of most people of both races in other areas continued largely unchanged. Even though I had now become a strong advocate for equal rights and was an active participant in the sit-ins and demonstrations, away from them, I still lived primarily by the old-established norms. George and I drove in his new car on our trip to the north, to Washington and Philadelphia, and finally to New York. We left with excitement and enthusiasm and almost no plans for what we would do or how things would be arranged. We spent the first night in a Washington suburb with some of George's relatives.

It was in an all-black middle-class neighborhood. I did not give it much thought initially, but there were probably only a few white people in the area. That evening I was sitting in the downstairs living room, and the doorbell rang. Since I was the only one in the room, I opened the door and encountered a black teenager. He was there to pick up one of the daughters of our host to go on a date.

I could tell I was completely not what he expected to see. I invited him in to wait while she finished getting ready, but after a few seconds, he declined and said he would come back later. That probably took an explanation by his date. That night we went with two of George's female relatives to a night club, the Black Beret, again in an all-black area, and I was the only white person in the club. It was great music and lots of fun. When I was in the bathroom, the guy standing next to me asked how I got there. I told him I came with some friends. He said that was pretty cool. I guess any two guys urinating together have at least one thing in common. The next night we stayed at the YMCA, which was closer to George Washington Hospital, the place where George had an interview the next morning. The following night was spent in Philadelphia, where he had an interview. The next day we arrived in New York. We did not know where we would be staying, so we drove to Times Square.

I found a big hotel there, so I had George let me out, and I went in and asked for a room for the night. The desk attendant told me I could not just show up at the best hotel on Times Square without a reservation and expect to get a room there. Where was I from? He did, however, have some consideration for two country boys from the south and found us a small room in the back part of the hotel.

The next day we tried the subway system for the first time and got lost somewhere in a distant part of the city. George eventually got to his hospital interview a bit late. Afterward, we drove back to Chapel Hill. It was a fun adventure, and I got to see things that made a lasting memory for me, both in the people we met and the places we went to. Later in life, George and I had many trips together, but this first one was something to remember. George was accepted for an internship at GW hospital in Washington and moved there. It would be a while before we met again.

The third and fourth years of medical school are clinical rotations. I was finished with the basic science and didactic classes. Students were then assigned to medical teams on the hospital wards. Each team was headed by an attending physician or professor in one of the branches of medicine, such as surgery or internal medicine or pediatrics. The teams consisted of residents who were specializing in that field and were at various levels in their training, and four to six medical students, either in their third or fourth year.

We would all be dressed in white coats of varying lengths depending on our status, and on the hospital rounds, we followed the professor in an orderly parade like a covey of albino quail. We would surround the patient, usually lying in their hospital bed and answer questions from the professor about the patient's status, hopefully with some accuracy. It was frequently stressful for the medical students and residents as well as the anxious patient being examined like a test subject. I tried to kill one of the first patients to whom I was assigned. He was already terminally ill with cancer that had spread throughout his body. The illness was not responding to any treatment. Early one morning, I was the first of my team to arrive on the hospital ward. The charge nurse took me to see the patient who was totally unresponsive and only breathing four to five times a minute. She asked what should be done.

When I reviewed his chart, I found the patient had received excessive doses of morphine, inconsistent with what would be required to control his pain. He was comatose from a drug overdose. I made the decision to resuscitate him with assisted breathing, but the attending physician called and told me not to do anything and let the disease take its course.

This was before the time when assisted suicide was openly discussed, but I had heard it did exist in the shadows of medical practice. I assumed, incorrectly as it turned out, that this was what was being done, and I asked the attending physician if I should continue to keep him on the regular morphine shots as ordered on his chart. He said no, so I instructed the nurse to do nothing else. Later in the day, I found out that the resident on the case had incorrectly written the morphine orders, which caused the coma. The patient slowly recovered from his accidental drug overdose, avoiding death for at least a little more time. It was an important moment when I realized how lives would depend on little decisions and details and mistakes in judgment or execution. An education in medicine involves a mixture of scientific facts, pseudoscientific folklore, social and ethically moral decisions, and managing people and expectations. It takes a long time to get there, and I was just starting.

I continued with the different medical specialties and subspecialties during the year with varying degrees of interest. I enjoyed the internal medicine rotations. I reluctantly tolerated the surgical assignments, partly because of the nature of the work and partly because of the professors who were usually borderline abusive to both the students and residents alike. I really disliked pediatrics. It was full of sick and crying babies. I also did not like psychiatry, which was full of sick and crying adults. It was apparent by then that I would never be an excellent medical student. I was always in the middle third of the class, not outstanding but also not in need of remediation. At times I wondered if I had the right temperament for the medical profession. Many of my classmates had the same questions. None of us seemed to be like Marcus Welby, MD. Would we like to do this for the rest of our lives? We joked that if we did not like taking care of live patients, we could be pathologists and take care of dead ones. Some of us did decide to do that.

In my third year of medical school, my friend Earl and I moved from the dormitory to an apartment in Carrboro, NC. It is a small town contiguous with Chapel Hill. It still had some of the old factories and mills and was a less expensive and more working-class neighborhood. We had a small upstairs apartment just off the main street where we lived until leaving the area.

I went to Washington for a few days to visit George. He was an intern then at George Washington University, where I had accompanied him a few months earlier for his interview. I met his new girlfriend and admired the new yellow Corvette he was driving around the highways of our capital. He had really moved on up from the small farm roads of Holly Springs and seemed very confident in his new situation. I was glad to see him so happy and successful. I still loved Chapel Hill and the social life and the athletics at Carolina. Despite the long hours required for study, I was able to get off for football games. We had parties on campus and at area clubs with entertainment provided by local bands like the "Hot Nuts" and by James Taylor, a guitar player and folk singer around Chapel Hill whose father was Dr. Issac Taylor, Dean of the Medical School.

The summer months between the third and fourth year of medical school was the last time I would have a traditional summer vacation with some extended time before starting the final year. I went to our family beach house in Kitty Hawk for a month. My grandfather had built this cottage in 1948 on beachfront property which he homesteaded by paying a year's worth of back taxes. At that time, this was a very remote area with few permanent residents, and it had not yet become OBX, one of the most famous and heavily populated ocean strands in the country. It was originally known for its historical significance since this was where in 1903 the Wright Brothers flew their flyer, the first heavier than air sustained powered flight in history. It was also a place that had never had a reported case of polio, a disease that was still causing summer epidemics in the south. We were taken to the beach house as young children where we spent the summer in relative isolation in an effort to prevent our getting the infection. We did not know this at the time and enjoyed the beach, but also missed our friends back in Ahoskie. We were each allowed to bring a friend from home for a week, and I always took Buzzy.

After that vacation, I spent a month as a guest student at Watts Hospital, a private community hospital in Durham, North Carolina. It was an opportunity to spend time with a physician in private practice and see how they delivered medical care. It was quite different than at the University Medical Center.

Most of the cases in Watts were not usually complex. The private patients were from a different social stratum than the very difficult or indigent patient treated at Carolina. I also saw a marked difference in the respect accorded to the physician. When the attending physician came on the ward, the nurses stood at attention and accompanied him everywhere, ready to provide him with just about anything he needed to help the patients. They still wore crisp starched white uniforms and caps. I was only an observer in this setting, but it was interesting to see one of the last places with this sort of traditional protocol in a passing era of medical etiquette. Afterward I returned to Chapel Hill to start my last year of training. I felt as though I was coming home to our little apartment in Carrboro, back with my friends and medical family.

In our fourth year of training, we were allowed to pick a few elective rotations that we wanted to try. I went to Moses Cone Hospital in Greensboro for a month in pediatrics and to Charlotte Memorial Hospital for a month of internal medicine. These hospitals were affiliated with UNC and provided me an opportunity to see practices in these areas. Some students chose these programs for their residency training when they left UNC.

I took a one-week elective rotation in the dermatology department. This was located in several small rooms somewhere in a remote area of the hospital. Dermatology was not a specialty that had appealed to me, and I had not expected to have any interest in this field. It did not have the excitement and high energy I was used to on the major surgical and medical wards. The department head was Clayton Wheeler, one of the pioneers in this field and author of the textbook we used. Dr. Wheeler was an example of a quiet professor who is a master in his field, and he made the subject extremely interesting even to students who had not considered it before. In a week, there is not an opportunity to learn with any depth of understanding such a complicated subject as the skin. I did not think I would go into dermatology, but he was the type of teacher who plants a seed in your brain that may germinate later.

Beckay had moved into an apartment near the place I shared with Earl. She was from South Carolina and came to UNC as a graduate student in art history. Her roommate, Rachel, was a girl that Earl had met and started dating. Beckay and I started spending some time together, which would eventually lead to the two of us dating as well. At first this was a matter of convenience, but as time passed, it changed into a more serious relationship.

I had dated a few girls in the past but none for very long or ever been in a serious relationship that became exclusive. After a year, it became apparent that any decisions we made about future plans might have to involve both of us. It was not that I had experienced then or at any time the fairy tale story of falling madly in love with someone at first sight. I did not think my own psychological makeup contained the gene for that particular phenomenon. But it was a new experience and an exciting time for me to have a partner who might become a permanent part of the rest of my life.

In our senior year medical students had to start looking for hospitals where we would go for our internship and residency training. We also had to decide what field of medicine we should pursue; for most of us, that would mean leaving Carolina. In those days, the medical faculty encouraged most students to go to other places for the next phase of their training so they could experience different ways of medical care and become well-rounded physicians.

A few of the top students would remain at UNC with the anticipation they would become faculty members someday. I was among the majority that would move somewhere else, but I did not have any definite plans. It was still difficult for me to know which specialty would be best for me. I decided I would stay in internal medicine since I had no interest in surgery or pediatrics or pathology. There are a large number of subspecialties in internal medicine, but I did not know which I would find the most rewarding. Cardiology was an exciting field and would always be in high demand and produce a large income.

Rheumatology was academically interesting, but the income was lower, and there were probably fewer opportunities for me there. None of the other fields had too much attraction for me. I did not have any desire to do research or publish papers, so I would not be at a major medical center. I enjoyed teaching some, but I did not think enough to make it a career.

I began by looking at some of the possible internships in the southeast since I had not yet thought of leaving the area. The schools at which I interviewed included Duke, our neighbor, and the biggest rival in sports. Duke and UNC are eight miles apart, so I would still be staying in the same area. After one interview with them, I knew I did not have the qualifications to get accepted there.

I interviewed at several other non-university affiliated places and still did not find any I liked. I continued looking farther south, and the last place I went turned out to be the best. The Medical College of Georgia in Augusta had taken several students from UNC in the past, and they spoke highly of it. After my visit there, I decided I would fit in well with their program. It was very much like Memorial Hospital in Chapel Hill. After meeting the faculty and touring with the residents, I was certain it was right for me. I met with the Chief of Medicine, and he said he liked me and encouraged me to come to MCG. The way the match for an internship works is that the students will list their top choices, and the hospital will list their top choices. On "match day," the pairings are announced, and everyone finds out where they will go. Outside arrangements are not supposed to be made before the match.

The Chief of medicine in Augusta told me they had twelve spots for their residency program, and if I had decided I would like to come, they would list me in their top twelve choices, if I would list MCG as my first choice. I told him I would like that and would list MCG as my top choice. So, I knew where I would be going for my internship. This type of arrangement was probably not strictly ethical, but as I learned from other students, it was not entirely unusual either. The arrangement worked out well for me. Augusta was not too far from Chapel Hill. That meant that Beckay and I could continue to see each other fairly conveniently. It was a difficult feeling when I left the campus, which had been home for the previous eight years. I visited my favorite places and people, reliving the memories I had made there. I expected I would not feel a similar allegiance to a new place, but I knew I would still have a close relationship with UNC for many years to come. They had paid for my education, and I owed them a lot of money for my student loans.

# Chapter 6

Internship and residency programs run each year from July 1 to June 30. In July 1969, I became Dr. G.T.Grigsby, a third-year internal medicine resident in Boston, MA, at the VA hospital on Huntington Avenue. I moved there to study with one of the outstanding physicians in renal disease. I was in the Tufts Medical School service. The Tufts University main teaching hospital is the New England Medical Center, where I also spent some time doing medical rotations. I had not been accepted into a planned renal fellowship, so I included as many rotations in the renal department as were available.

Washington DC summers can be uncomfortably hot, so I welcomed a cooler summer in Boston. Neither my bright yellow Corvette nor my new Boston apartment was air-conditioned. I loaded a U-Haul truck with all my Washington possessions and drove it to Boston. My girlfriend followed me in the Corvette. We began the move on a Saturday morning and arrived in the late evening in Boston. My new apartment was at the corner of Boylston and Tremont, which was located on the edge of the "combat zone." This was an easy walk to the New England Medical Center. When I had to go to the VA hospital, I could walk across the street to Boston Common and catch the MTA, which would let me out in front of the VA on Huntington Avenue. I found Boston to be less friendly in general than Washington. Traffic and their traffic circles were more difficult. The rules for navigating the Boston circles seemed to be the opposite of the DC rules.

Parking was a nightmare. Not only was there double parking, but there was also triple parking. Even pay for parking was hard to find and when found was expensive. On one occasion my girlfriend and I were refused admission into a restaurant. I do not know the real reason, but they said it was because her mini-skirt was too short. I doubted that.

Like Washington, Boston is filled with historical landmarks, great art galleries, museums, and fine restaurants. The museums were not free as I had become accustomed to in D.C. Boston is small enough to be a walkable city, and the Freedom Trail is a great path through historical sites. After finishing my year in Boston, I was ready to begin my military obligation as the Berry Plan for recruiting physicians in the armed services had mandated. I was fortunate that my enlistment schedule had allowed my completion of an internal medicine residency without military interruption. This would allow me to enter the service as a specialist instead of a general medical office and possibly get a more desirable assignment. It was July 1970, and I was now Captain George Talmadge Grigsby, MD, a newly inducted officer in the US Air Force and was beginning my military service at Forbes Air Force Base in Topeka, Kansas. I had not been to Topeka but knew a little bit about it.

I knew the famous Menninger Foundation was there and that my friend and basketball coach from Chapel Hill, Dean Smith, had graduated from Topeka High School. The US Supreme Court decision of 1954 Brown v. Board of Education of Topeka was well known to many blacks. I also knew they had a lot of tornados in Kansas.

I had spent two weeks in basic training at Sheppard Air Force Base in Wichita Falls, Texas, where I learned basic military skills and how to handle firearms. When I reached Forbes I became the Chief of the Internal Medicine Department, a position I would hold for the full two years of my military service. Forbes was a rather small TAC (Tactical Air Command) base without a lot of medical specialists, so

I had a lot of responsibility for problematic patients. The flight surgeons sent me difficult cases, especially pilots with questionable cardiac arrhythmias. This was crucial for the pilots who knew my decision might ground them from flying, and medical consultation with me could cause them a lot of anxiety.

I had an outstanding group of corpsmen. They could assist with the evaluation of patients, suturing of injuries, and most of them were career enlisted men and knew how to navigate the military system. They and their friends in other departments could usually get things done quickly and avoid the official roadblocks.

The black personnel appeared happy to receive medical care from a black physician, and I was unaware of any other patients or personnel who found it to be a problem. All the other doctors were white and professionally and socially we were all a close group. We enjoyed meeting at the officers' club, which had excellent food and was better than at many of the local restaurants in town. Occasionally we would visit Kansa City, known for the excellent barbecue restaurants, and for longer trips, we would go skiing in Vail, Colorado. The return trip from Vail was sometimes delayed when I-70 would be closed because of heavy blizzards. Blizzards and tornadoes were just part of living in Kansas. The economy of Topeka was heavily dependent on the military base, but the air force personnel themselves were not always embraced by the residents. Black service members were sometimes denied rentals in some of the local apartment complexes. The landlords that did this could be placed off-limits by the air force.

I found an apartment about a fifteen-minute drive from the base. I met my neighbor, Dr. J Barry Claycomb, who was starting his psychiatry residency at the Menninger Foundation. He had just finished medical school at Indiana University. After becoming friends, we decided that staying at the Gatehouse Apartments was not the best living arrangement Topeka had to offer.

We wanted a house with a swimming pool, and we found one for sale in a prestigious area on Lake Sherwood. It was a smaller house than most in the development but was located directly on the lake. We had a realtor, so we toured the house and made an offer that was accepted. Since Barry and I were both physicians, we felt there would be no difficulty qualifying for a loan. We tried to assume the mortgage that was in place, but the lender refused to accept that. After looking for loans from a number of banks and savings and loan companies and being refused, it became very clear that there was a problem. Being black, I was the problem. Barry was white, but being a first-year psychiatry resident, his salary was not enough for him to qualify for a mortgage.

Our realtor advised us to completely pay off the original house loan, and then we could search for a new mortgage. It would be at a higher rate but could be obtained. Finding that much money was a stretch for Barry and me, but we did it. In July 1971, we moved into the new house on the lake. A few days later, I had a patient who lived at Lake Sherwood excitedly tell me that Lake Sherwood was no longer all white.

A black had just moved across the street from her and was directly on the lake. I smiled and told her it was I. Most of the surrounding neighbors were always friendly; however, when Barry and I applied for membership in the Sherwood Lake Club, we were always denied. We had looked forward to putting our sailfish in the lake.

A month after our moving into Lake Sherwood, a family, Dana and Sue Anderson moved next door. Barry and I could not have asked for more desirable neighbors. Years later, I learned from Dana that his realtor had offered to release him from his house purchase because he would have a black neighbor. Dana declined and became one of my best friends for many years. He is a Kansas University alumnus, and he and Sue are some of their biggest supporters. There are two buildings on campus named after the Dana Anderson Family and a private Anderson Box at the football stadium. He still invites me to join him there for the games and does not hold it against me that I am a graduate of Carolina, one of KUs biggest basketball rivals.

Barry and I both enjoyed skiing, and in 1973 we purchased a condominium in Aspen, Colorado. When we were looking for a place to buy, I asked our realtor if she knew of any other black residents in town. She thought for a minute but was unaware of any, although she thought there might be a black caterer. We got our condo, and there was not any problem obtaining loan financing. It was a beautiful place at the bottom of Ajax, the local name for the Aspen Mountain Ski area. In those days, the skiing was great, and there was not yet any snowboarders. I was discharged from the air force in 1972 and began an emergency department practice at Stormont Vail Hospital in Topeka. I was the first physician there but was soon joined by L. Wayne Capooth, who had been a flight surgeon colleague at Forbes AFB. Afterward, Wayne and I moved to Memorial Hospital, which was a smaller department where we stayed for two years.

In 1981 he returned to his home town of Memphis, Tennessee, and I accepted a position in the emergency department at Southern Nevada Memorial Hospital in Las Vegas, Nevada. This was a city where I could work as a physician and also begin my new career as a professional blackjack player. I soon learned I could not survive as a gambler. So, I remained working as a physician except for a hiatus when I returned to North Carolina.

Not long after arrival in Las Vegas, I saw a sign on Charleston Blvd on which appeared in large lettering Lucius Blanchard, MD. I was certain that I knew this person from UNC. I gave a call to the office number and told the receptionist who I was and asked to speak to the doctor. When he took my call, he seemed to not know who I was, which I thought was strange, but he said if I came to the office the following day, he would take me to lunch. I decided to go.

DR. GEORGE T. GRIGSBY AND DR. LUCIUS BLANCHARD

# Chapter 7

The Medical College of Georgia in Augusta would be my home and training program for the next two years. The hospital, much like the one at UNC, was a referral center for the uninsured or the sickest patients in that part of the state. Complicated or difficult or seriously ill patients were sent there. The building was old with multiple patient rooms and wards and long dark corridors connecting different parts of the medical complex. Some of the special services, such as the ICU and CCU, were in areas that were small but well-equipped and staffed.

The community around the hospital center was much different than at Chapel Hill. The hospital in Augusta was adjacent to an inner-city low-income housing project and near businesses and stores that were there to serve that community. The area was not considered safe, and we were careful to be aware of our surroundings when arriving at or leaving the hospital. There were some familiar faces present. Three of the first-year internal medicine interns had also come here from UNC, so I knew some other people on the residency staff. One of the faculty members was a prior UNC medical graduate that I knew well. The Medical College was also associated with the Augusta VA Hospital, and part of our residency was spent in that location. I found an inexpensive apartment in a better section of town about thirty minutes from the medical center. Bill was one of my fellow students from UNC and was also doing his training at MCG. He was renting in the same complex, so I did know one person in the place where I lived. Appropriately, the apartment house was across the street from a golf course.

Augusta is famous for the Master's Golf Tournament. I am not a golfer, but in Augusta even non-participants become part of the sport in some fashion, and several of my friends were regulars on the golf course. I bought a set of used clubs from the pro shop for sixty dollars. Sometimes late in the afternoon on summer days, I would sneak onto the last few golf holes on the course across from my apartment building and practice a few shots. I took some lessons from the pro there and played several rounds of golf but found I had neither the time nor the talent or the interest to be a successful golfer.

The first year of internship for a doctor is an intense period of hands-on training in their chosen field. I was in the internal medicine program, which required taking care of the most complex and difficult cases in the hospital. Teams were assigned with a resident in his second or third year of training, one or two first-year interns, and several medical students. An attending physician would be in charge and make rounds with the group and check on our patients, but the minute to minute decisions were usually made by the resident team. The intern and a first-year resident also stay in the hospital overnight on-call three to four times a week and are responsible for anything that has to be done immediately.

As an intern and resident, you learn primarily from observation and repeating what the senior staff has done. You watch and learn from their decisions. While most times the outcomes are good, part of that education is seeing the results of those decisions that in a few cases go terribly and fatally wrong. Part of the education of a physician is that most of them, at some time in their career, will make errors that will result in the death of a patient.

As a student, there is some insolation from that. Even though the student was a team participant in making an error that caused a bad result and the student feels the regret and sorrow intensely, there is some solace in that he alone could not have made the mistake. Every student has seen these things happen to patients. Some mistakes just happen inadvertently and some by the inexperience of the provider directing the medical care.

You cannot be insulated from this. One day you are an observing medical student. The next day you are the person in charge of your patients and teaching the new medical students on your team. The immediate responsibility is always stressful since there are frequently times when you alone have to make the right call. In some situations, the residents are the only ones immediately available to handle extreme issues such as cardiac arrests, respiratory failures, or septic shock, all of which can be fatal if not handled quickly and correctly.

I was prepared as well as possible since I had trained in an excellent medical center, and I had been an attentive, although not an outstanding pupil. I was fortunate during my residency training that I only made a few errors of major consequence and rarely contributed to my patients' death. I did well as a member of the house staff and was highly regarded by the teachers and the Chief attending of the medical service. That was something that I appreciated and would become more important in the future in an unexpected way.

My relationship with Beckay was in a hiatus of sorts. While we both anticipated we would still be together, I did not invite her to move from Chapel Hill to Augusta to live with me. So there was some uncertainty about what would happen when we were living apart. She was ready for marriage and children, and I was still not so sure that was what I wanted. She visited me when I was not on call at the hospital, and the relationship continued with her expectation that we would get married. I dated a few other girls during this period, but no one with whom I had a serious relationship.

Eventually, Beckay and I decided we would make it an official engagement and planned to get married the next year. My income as a resident was barely enough to cover my living expenses, so I told her I could not afford both an engagement ring and a television set, and since football season was starting, I gave her an engagement TV. I was then a dedicated Washington Redskins fan. As a teenager, I had met Eddie LeBaron when he was the quarterback for the

Washington Redskins and visited Ahoskie on a publicity tour. It was the only autograph I ever collected.

While I was in Georgia, I made several weekend trips back to Chapel Hill. I went to visit my old roommate Earl and to some football games and to see the places where I used to hang out with friends. It had not been a long time since I had left, but it was not the same experience. The campus was still familiar and beautiful as ever, but most of the people I knew had also moved on, and there was no relationship with the teachers with whom I use to spend time. Even after such a short absence, as a famous Tar Heel once said, "you can't go home again."

I enjoyed my time at the Medical College of Georgia. Since it was a public teaching hospital, the resident staff was given a lot of responsibility for the care of patients, and we usually performed with diligence and thoroughness. It is exciting and rewarding to be presented with complicated and difficult medical cases and use your newly developing skills in diagnosis and treatment and see the expected good results in most outcomes.

The attending staff was comprised of excellent teachers who treated us as valuable colleagues. They gave us tickets to the early rounds of the Master's Golf Tournament when they were not going to use them, and we got to see the best golfers in the world in what some people think is the best golf tournament played. I think their attitude had some correlation with being from a smaller southern town where gentility was still practiced, and respect and politeness were expected.

In accordance with this period in time, our attending staff and the resident staff were still all white except for several Asian foreign medical school graduates and teachers. The patient clientele was a general mix of all patients, but the indigent people of color tended to be the sickest and most complex patients. This was partly because of poor treatment in their community and partly due to the difficulty in their getting access to medical care. By the time many of them were admitted to our medical service they had received either no care or ineffective treatment. It was common for them to be severely ill with multiple problems involving multiple organ systems.

Providing care for them was complex and time-consuming. The residents had two informal awards we gave ourselves. One was the Black Cloud award, given to the resident who had the most numerous and unfortunate bad luck events during the week. The other was the SNOW award, given to the resident who had admitted the Sickest Negro of the Week. The nineteen sixties were bringing about changing attitudes in racial sensitivity, but that work would remain ongoing. The attitude we showed then was wrong in any time period and changing that would be part of gaining humility, experience, and maturity on our part.

I started as a second-year resident in July of 1969. I rotated on the clinical wards and in some of the specialty clinics and in the emergency room. At that time, there was no limit to the number of hours a resident could work, and we were usually at the hospital for thirty-six hours on duty and had twelve hours off to sleep and recover. In addition to that, we had required reading and sometimes research. In the second year, we were allowed to take some elective rotations on the medical service. For one elective, I chose dermatology, which seemed to exist in its own separate medical world.

Then and to some extent, still now, dermatology was a small specialized area that was not a well-integrated part of any other medical department. It was not greatly attractive to most residents. In fact, I mainly requested this elective to get some rest and relaxation for a month. But as I got involved in the field, I discovered that dermatology was not just syphilis, pimples, rashes and warts but actually a mixture of medicine and cutaneous surgery and pathology and many new areas of research. The skin is the largest organ in the body, and there are hundreds of diseases that can affect it. Many of them are not well understood even today. The complex reactions that occur in the skin may affect the entire body in many ways.

Dermatology residents came to work about eight in the morning and left by five. They always had time for lunch and almost never got called in at night. They were the happiest residents in the training I had met. To some extent, I missed the excitement of the immediate and critical care of patients, but I began to realize that in the long run that could lead to rapid physician burn out and dissatisfaction with life in general. I talked with the head of the department about becoming a dermatology resident and he encouraged me to think about it seriously. I put it in my mind as an avenue to explore, but I still had the rest of my internal medicine year to finish. The day after I left dermatology, I was assigned to the gastrointestinal ward. The first patient I admitted that day was an extremely critical GI bleeder. He was a chronic alcoholic with severe cirrhosis of the liver and dilated veins in his esophagus that had ruptured and were bleeding profusely.

I worked all night on him with medications and blood transfusions and gastric lavages and compression tubes to try to stabilize him. About four in the morning the bleeding and the shock were controlled. He was finally past the critical stage. I was still in the hospital the next day, getting ready to care for another group of patients to be evaluated for difficult problems and knew that I might be there another night as well.

I thought about the friends I had made on the dermatology service and how they would all be sleeping at home and looking forward to another normal day in their clinic. I knew I would be with my patient again and that he would be bleeding again, and even if I was successful in his recovery again this time, he would be back with the same condition and it would be fatal sometime soon. My work was rewarding for the short term but I did begin to seriously consider what kind of career I wanted for the rest of my life.

Beckay and I got married in Columbia, South Carolina that year. That was where most of her family lived and where she was working as a teacher. I had suggested we wait, but she wanted to go ahead with the plans we had started. We had a short honeymoon for a weekend on Grand Bahama Island. Then it was back to training for me, and she finished her teaching assignment in Columbia and moved to Augusta.

In May of 1970, I and some of my friends stood on top of the hospital where I was working that night and watched as the downtown area of Augusta burned in a race riot. A teenage black man had been arrested by the police and jailed, where he was tortured and killed in prison. The black population responded with riots and burning. Lester Maddox, the governor of Georgia and a strong segregationist, called in the National Guard who shot and killed some of the unarmed protestors. The fires and riots lasted for several days. The situation was reminiscent of the riots in Watts five years earlier, but I had not expected this to happen in Georgia. The era of non-violent, sit-in demonstrations that began in Greensboro was coming to an end, and the hardening of race relations was beginning. Watching from the top of the building, it was frightening to see a historic southern town burn like this and to know there would be similar events in the years to come.

After several days the rioters dispersed, partly through the mediating efforts of singer James Brown, a former Augusta resident and the Godfather of Soul. This black man urged all sides to start communicating with each other. The riots ended but not the tension that had been building for years. Later the prison guards were acquitted of any wrongdoing.

When I had been a medical student at UNC, we would sometimes watch the news at night while on call at the hospital and not busy. I followed the story of the Vietnam War with much interest since I would have been considered an anti-war activist and did march occasionally in protests. I remember thinking at the time that the war would soon be over and would not involve me personally, especially since I had draft deferments as a medical student and intern and resident. So, my concern about the war was real but also not personal since I did not anticipate ever being directly involved. I had never considered a career in the military or that I was suited in any way to serve in that capacity. That all changed as I neared the end of my two years at MCG. During my first year as an intern the US Army instituted the Berry Plan to bring physicians into the military. There was a need for more doctors in the service since the United States had started the big military build-up in Vietnam.

Medical residents were given a two-year deferment and then usually subject to being drafted as an enlisted man or voluntarily enlisting as a medical officer. During my second year of residency, I received notice that I would be joining the US Army in July of 1970, and after basic training at Fort Sam Houston in San Antonio, Texas I would be assigned for a year somewhere in Vietnam as a Captain in the US Army Medical Corps.

Greetings from your Uncle Sam: You are in the army now.

# Chapter 8

I finished my last rotation on the internal medicine team at the Medical College of Georgia in July of 1970. Several of my fellow residents were also going into the military, so we had our farewell party with mixed emotions. We were leaving the comfortable lifestyle we knew and going somewhere none of us had anticipated and had no experience.

The nightly news from Vietnam had become an obsession with the American public. Photographs and film clips showed the dead and wounded soldiers on both sides of the war and an endless carnage of civilians caught in the middle. All this had produced an entrenched divide in the public's opinion about the war. It was a divide based on age and conscience and fueled by patriotism and politics.

The warnings from the politicians of the domino effect as "yellow communism" moved into the Indochina peninsular was met with cries and chants of "Hell, no, we won't go!" I did not know anyone who had actually defected to Canada to avoid the draft, but they were on the nightly news, and they looked a lot like me. At that time I still had long wavy hair and a handlebar mustache and the attitude from the protest generation. I thought, as did most of my generation, the war to be immoral and senseless, but I did not seriously consider avoiding the draft. I was not from a military background, and no one from my immediate family had been in the military service since one of my relatives had been an officer in the Confederate Army and had stolen an entire train. At least that was what I heard from my family historians. Whether that was true or not, I still felt some southern male obligation to serve my country even though I did not agree with their actions. I took some comfort in the fact that as a doctor, I would probably never have to actually kill anyone.

I went by the dermatology department to let the Chief, Dr. Smith know that I was still interested in having a residency there and asked if he would consider accepting me when I finished my time in the service. He was amenable to my plan and asked me to get in touch with him when I was ready to be separated from the army. I thought this could work out well for me and began preparing for my military service.

In the rush of getting people to combat readiness, there was a program to train second lieutenants in three months.

They were the "ninety-day wonders" in the eyes of the well trained and experienced career officers and sergeants who were the backbone of the US Army. We were the six weeks doctors since that was the amount of training time we received, and then we were commissioned as Captains or Majors as soon as we were inducted.

My basic training took place at Fort Sam Houston in San Antonio, Texas. My wife Beckay and I drove there from Augusta with a stopover for a few days in the French Quarter in New Orleans for some fun and excitement before I took the oath of office. I found an apartment in San Antonio that would house us for the duration and prepared to learn the basic skills a rookie soldier would need.

The basic training was not particularly rigorous since the drill sergeants and course instructors were aware that many of us were of advanced age when compared to the usual recruit who averaged nineteen years old. We were not required to perform any strenuous physical activity. There was an hour of formation drilling in the morning, which was comical. Here is one of our marching questions. You are drilling a line of men and the next step they take will put them over a cliff. How do you stop them? You cannot say "Halt!" since that command requires another step. The answer is, "Gas!". This would require the troops to stop immediately and put on their gas mask. I learned useful things like this and spent a few minutes in a chemical weapons simulation chamber where I learned how to respond to the "Gas" command.

We trained in the field for three days, where we were introduced to live-fire exercises and required to fire a few rounds from an M-16 rifle with an instructor almost holding our hands. We were not allowed to load any ammunition or to disassemble the weapon and were not given any training in hand grenades, which I found disappointing. As kids, Buzzy and I were frequent but usually unsuccessful hunters, and we mixed a lot of gunpowder to blow up things.

We had a night exercise where we had to navigate through a field a mile long. There were snipers who would occasionally open fire on us with machine guns and tracer ammunition that looked like fireworks. The most dangerous part of that night's exercise was when I tripped over a dead cow. I was not really hurt, though. The basic training experience was not much more rigorous than some of the scout camps and hiking expeditions Buzzy and I had done as Boy Scouts. San Antonio was an interesting town, and there was enough time for my wife and me to see the Alamo, which was smaller than I expected, and to enjoy the restaurants and music clubs on the River Walk. We took a weekend trip to Mexico and did a little shopping and sightseeing in the border towns.

When basic training was over, I was given a one week leave and told to report to the airport in San Francisco for my deployment to Vietnam. My wife took me to the airport. We said goodbye as they directed me onto the airplane. I was anxious about what would happen when I arrived in Vietnam but had also begun to develop a sense of positive anticipation regarding this new period in my life.

Many hours later we landed at Tan Son Nhat airport outside of Saigon and were transferred to temporary quarters. Here we were briefed and given basic physicals and vaccinations. I got to see some of Saigon, a beautiful city with very little evidence of the war in which the people were engaged. At this time, the fighting was still in the countryside, villages, and rural provinces. After a few days, I learned I was being assigned to the 23rd Infantry, which was more commonly known as the Americal Division. It was headquartered in Chu Lai, which was in the northern part of South

Vietnam. Along with a lot of other new soldiers, I was flown to the airport in Chu Lai and transferred to the Combat Center for my first real in-country training experience. This was my introduction to how a combat zone looked. Of course, it was nothing like Saigon. The camp was cut into the beaches and hills extending up from the South China Sea.

The entire base extended for many miles. It was surrounded by wire fences and patrolled by guards at multiple layers. Observation towers were located along the beaches to watch the ocean for enemy invaders, and on the land perimeter toward the mountains overlooking the base. I was billeted in a four-man tent along with several other new officers. We were sent to the quartermaster who gave us the camouflage fatigues we would wear and the appropriate insignia showing name, rank, and in which segment we served. According to my designation, I was L Blanchard, a Captain in the Medical Corps, assigned to the Americal Division. We spent several weeks training in the combat center. I learned how to detect booby traps on the jungle trails. These were tripwires, punji sticks, and toe poppers, which were traps hidden under the leaves and brush. We learned how ambush situations would develop and to never chase retreating Vietcong soldiers since there would usually be a secondary ambush waiting. Never follow the same jungle trail twice. Always board a Huey helicopter from the downhill side.

I was taught how to recognize land mine fields. If you were not sure where the enemy land mines were buried, get a local villager and send him out to walk in first. He might know. We had instruction on dealing with the Vietnamese civilians and their national army, known as ARVN soldiers. Relationships with them were important since part of our mission was to win the hearts and minds of the local people. That would turn out to be even more difficult than winning the shooting war. One of my impressions from the combat training center in Chu Lai was how young and how black the new recruits were. Most of them were just out of high school and had no way to get college deferments. They had no political connections that could get them in the National Guard and no medical connections who could document a physical condition that would get them out of the military requirement. They were drafted, rapidly trained, and deployed, and many swiftly became casualties. The greatest number of men killed were the new recruits belonging to the 19 to 21-year-old category. Just as in previous conflicts, it was old men sending young men to do the fighting and dying. I made a good friend while in the combat training center. His name was Ben and he was the physician assigned there to provide any medical care needed by the new recruits.

He was serving as a general medical officer but was planning to go into dermatology when he finished his military service. He had already been accepted at the University of North Carolina dermatology program after his discharge. That was exactly what I was hoping to do. We talked a lot, and I picked up some ideas that I thought might help me later. After we got to be good friends, he told me a story about himself. He had originally been assigned to a field unit when he first came to the Americal Division. Then on one of their combat missions, he shot down the helicopter in which he was flying. Before boarding a helicopter, the passengers are supposed to clear their weapons, which means removing any ammunition from the firing chamber so there could be no accidental discharges. Ben had a .45 caliber sidearm which he tried to clear after taking off. When he attempted to remove the round from the firing chamber, the pistol discharged and sent the bullet through the floor of the helicopter and damaged the control cables. No one was hurt, and the aircraft was able to rotate to the ground safely. Ben was reprimanded and transferred to this new position. So I guess there is a good reason they did not let doctors handle weapons in our basic training camp.

After my training in the Combat Center, I was going to be assigned to a position somewhere in the Americal Division. There were generally three areas of assignment. There were established hospitals that were permanent well-equipped units staffed by fully trained teams of physicians and surgeons. These were on the larger and more secure permanent bases. In more remote locations, there were facilities for treating less severely injured or ill patients. These clearing stations were staffed by several doctors and medics and a variety of support staff. They had a small number of hospital beds in a clinic setting. The most remote assignment was with a field unit on a firebase. These were small facilities, usually in a tent, where a unit was stationed and which could move as necessary. There would usually be a general doctor and a medic assigned to these units to treat simple conditions or any severe problems that could not be quickly transferred to a major hospital setting. One of the most successful operations in Vietnam was the speed with which a medical evacuation helicopter could transport a wounded soldier from the field to a fully equipped hospital. There were a few other unique medical assignments at other levels too.

Another new medical officer and I were up for placement at the same time. Two positions needed to be filled. One was on a firebase in a tent in the jungle and the other a physician who would be attached to the headquarters division in Chu Lai. This latter involved mainly caring for the senior army staff as well as some administrative work. The other physician was above me in time in grade by two weeks, so he would get the headquarters job and I, the firebase. However, he failed his physical and was detained for further testing. I was given the headquarters assignment, which was considered one of the best possible places to be based. My role at division headquarters was very easy. In the morning I would see a few patients from division command at sick call for routine medical problems. Occasionally I would be called to the quarters of a high-ranking general officer for their medical issues. My other task was to review and answer inquiries from politicians or other public officials about the health of one of their constituents in the service, usually in an attempt to get them returned to the States on a medical issue.

I was also responsible for treating the lifers- those officers who were making the Army their career- for any venereal disease they might have acquired and for making sure the medical record confirmed that the penicillin they received was for a common cold. There were no patients that I had to see for urgent or emergency conditions.

My living facilities were comfortable with an air-conditioned office and sleeping quarters and hot showers. I had an aide to handle any administrative problems and drive me anywhere I needed to go. I was a few blocks away from the Division officers club where I could spend the afternoons drinking a beer for ten cents in military pay script, get a steak or lobster dinner for a dollar or go to the PX to shop for anything I might possibly need. After two months, I asked my commanding officer if there were any other assignment I could get. I found there was an open position at a medical clearing station. It was still in the Division headquarters area close to where I was currently assigned. This was a company of about one hundred soldiers, four physicians, and about sixty hospital beds for the early or intermediate level of medical care.

I put in my request and got moved to that assignment. I would spend the rest of my time in Vietnam with the 23rd Medical Battalion at Headquarters Company A. Except for periods of TDY, which were temporary duty assignments in other locations, this became my home in Vietnam.

I was with two other general medical physicians and a psychiatrist in our company. Gary was a general surgeon and a higher-ranking officer. There was a full Colonel in charge, but he was seldom on the premises. Randy was a general medical doctor and was planning to go into dermatology, just as I was. He was going to join the residency program at the University of Michigan after discharge. I was billeted in a nice three-man hut with two other officers. One was the head of the clerical staff and went by the name "Mad Dog John." The other was the officer in charge of the motor pool and called "Son of a Bitch Turbovitch." I got named "Cool Hand Luke" after a famous movie character. Like me, they were in the service for a limited time, and none of us acted like regular army. In the mornings we had sick call for any routine medical problems. The afternoons were reserved for surgical procedures such as cleaning or suturing minor injuries from gunshot or shrapnel wounds.

On some days we would be on diversionary call and receive a large number of casualties. I taught Mad Dog and Son of a Bitch basic surgery assistant skills, and sometimes all of us would be managing wounded soldiers in the operating theater. For much of the time we were on stand-down status and free to visit the officer's club in the afternoons and evenings.

Two of the most common problems we treated at sick call were venereal diseases and drug addiction. Sexual contacts were readily available and inexpensive anywhere in the country. Drugs such as marijuana and heroin could be found almost anyplace. Sometimes it was hard to grasp that even in the middle of an active combat zone, a soldier could easily get laid and high. We had a number of repeat customers who were not overly bright and never seemed to remember the army instructional video they saw regarding "VD and You." One of the somewhat dubious behavioral modification techniques we used played into a popular misconception held by the enlisted men. There was a rumor that if a soldier caught a venereal disease called the "Black Syph," he could never be cured and would not be allowed to return to the States. There was a mythical army base hidden in the jungles of Thailand where infected soldiers would be sent for an indefinite period.

Sometimes when a recurring VD patient was in the clinic, the medics and I would go into a nearby room and discuss loudly enough that the patient could hear that it was possible he had the "Black Syph" and how we might have to send him to Thailand. Then we would return and tell the frightened and credulous patient there was one more drug he could take that might work, but he would have to be more careful in the future. It is doubtful that this changed anyone's behavior, but it was fun for us and maybe helped in a few cases. There was a constant use of drugs in our company, primarily by the enlisted men. As the officers of our company, we were directed from command to have in place a program to reduce the drug problem. None of us had any strong desire to enforce this as an imperative objective since we knew our primary mission was to provide medical care for the wounded soldiers and get them back into service as quickly as possible. Our solution was to have an occasional drug raid on the enlisted men's quarters and confiscate any drugs we found. Usually, it was only marijuana we discovered.

This did temporarily reduce drug use in our camp, and we could send a report that a large number of drugs were confiscated and destroyed. It also gave the officers a free source of pot if we wanted to smoke it occasionally. We did not charge the men with any criminal offenses since that would be counterproductive in achieving our mission. It was a solution that seemed to make everyone happy, especially the officers.

After I had spent some time in service, I was eligible to request leave for a week. In the military that is like getting a vacation where the Army tells you where you can go, what you can do, and if you do not return on time, they can put you in jail. The soldier is issued a set of orders detailing all of these rules and obligations. He must keep this in his possession at all times and produce it if requested by any authorities. I did not know where I would take my leave. I went to the airport and requested the destination of the next flight for soldiers getting leave and then asked to be put on that airplane.

As an officer, I was placed ahead of any enlisted men waiting to board. I was soon on a flight to Hong Kong.

# Chapter 9

It is a tale told thousands of times; in the ancient city of Troy and the Tudor court of Henry the Eighth; on the Shakespearian stage and in the Hollywood movie "Casablanca." In my story, she was Terri, or at least that was the Anglicized version of her Chinese name. She was not classically beautiful by western standards, but she was definitely Asian cute.

Not cute like a Kewpie Doll; like an enchanting Anime actress. I would spend as much time with her as possible in the coming months, sometimes even with the danger of possible arrest and jail. Dangerous, immediate and total attractions can occur and be remembered for a lifetime, just as it happened to Henry the Eighth in London, to Rick Blaine in World War Two in Paris and to me in Hong Kong.

I did not have any plans for what I would do or where I would stay in Hong Kong. I met a few soldiers on the plane and said I would look them up while I was on leave and we would do something together. There was a reception center for servicemen at the airport to help us get oriented. I asked them for lodging somewhere in the middle of town where everything would be close, so they got me a room at a hotel and arranged for a taxi to take me there. One of my new friends decided to stay there also, so we rode together. As we were checking in, I passed a group of young girls going through the lobby to the hotel restaurant and casually said good morning, as we are accustomed to doing in the south.

After I carried my luggage up to the room, I came back down to eat at the restaurant. The girls were still there and when they saw I was alone, one asked if I would like to join them at their table. I am usually very shy with girls I do not know and would ordinarily decline, but since this was a unique experience, I accepted the offer.

I assumed that Asian girls could be interested in American men since we might be a bit of a curiosity to them even though many soldiers came there on leave. All of them seemed to be in their mid-twenties, were well educated and worked in various hotels or shops in the downtown area. I asked about things to do in Hong Kong since I was not interested in just hanging out in bars. One of the girls, who said her name was Terri, said I should come to the USO center that night. It was close to my hotel and they were having dinner and a get-acquainted party for US servicemen. I thought that sounded like a good place to start my vacation.

When I arrived at the USO club there were a lot of people there, many of them soldiers on leave, as well as a number of local girls. Terri was there as a USO hostess and still with some of her friends. She greeted me and asked how I was doing and if there was anything I needed. I was trying to find the hotel where a friend of mine who was also on leave in Hong Kong was staying. So, I said yes there was, "I need to find an address."

She looked at me with quizzical Asian eyes and a quizzical Asian smile and said, "why do you need a dress?". My southern English meets her BBC English. For the rest of the evening, we spent all the time together. We talked and dined and danced. I convinced her I never wear dresses. People under great stress or emotion describe having tunnel vision. That was my experience in that Terri was all that I could see, and everything else was pushed to the edges and blurred out of focus and experience. She was all that I can remember from that party. Afterward, we went out to the street and walked for a while, looking into shops and store windows. The whole city experience of lights, smells, sounds, colors, and people surrounded us. It was my first night in the center of Hong Kong. I have always liked Asian places, and people and this exposure was even more intense than I had anticipated. It seemed so much more vibrant with Terri holding my arm and walking quietly with me; it was as though we had done this before.

Terri said she would have to go home, and she called a taxi to pick her up. She told me she worked at the American Express office in a local hotel, and said I could come to see her tomorrow. Definitely. Then she kissed me good night; it was as though we had done this before.

It was late at night as I walked back to my hotel. I wondered what if anything might happen when I went to her American Express office the next day. Maybe it would be nothing. Romance for one night may fade in the morning sun. In the meantime, it was exciting being in Hong Kong in the evening and seeing all the life on the streets. In the few blocks I walked, I found I could be measured for a tailored suit immediately and have a fitting done the next day. Another store would design custom-fit shoes using an outline of my feet and have them ready in the morning. Almost any type of food was available, some of which looked to still be alive. I could easily find a new friend to spend the night with me if I wanted or even two. I was offered sunglasses that would make me look high fashion and enough electronics at bargain prices to equip a music studio. I stopped in the bar in my hotel for a while and had a Bloody Mary and let the experiences of the first day settle into a memorable pattern. I slept well that night, even hearing the loud noises from the street. They did not keep me awake like the sounds of incoming rockets and artillery fire.

The next morning, I went to see the tailor who would make me a suit. I did not need a tailor-made suit, especially since I was returning to Vietnam, but it seemed irresponsible to be in Hong Kong and not get one made. I picked out material that turned out to look better on the rack than on me and got measured and told to return the next day. The late morning was spent looking around Kowloon and the harbor. After lunch, I went to the American Express office. Terri was working there and seemed happy to see me. We talked a few minutes, reliving the previous evening and talking about her city and what I might do there.

Then she suggested I come back after she got off work so I could join her and several friends and they would take me to a local restaurant that night. It sounded fun and I agreed to meet her later. I began to wonder if Chinese girls always traveled in groups, and to some extent, as I was to learn later, that was correct.

After she finished work, Terri and I, along with five or six of her friends, walked from the hotel to the waterfront. We went to a family-style restaurant overlooking the harbor. The water reflected all the lights of the city in rippling waves and patterns. A constant stream of shipping moved through the channel separating the peninsular from Hong Kong Island.

Music played from the evening dinner cruise boats moving slowly around the coastline. We could see people dancing or standing along the rails enjoying the evening. The food was varied and local, and there were enough familiar dishes that I had an excellent dinner over several hours. Terri was upset that I over tipped the waiter, and she tried unsuccessfully to get the money back from him. What can I say? American soldiers on leave are generous. Later in the evening all of us walked back uptown. I recognized several of the guys who had been on the flight from Vietnam with me, but

I did not invite them to join us. I could tell they were wondering what I was doing with all these young women following me along the street. To some extent, I was wondering the same thing, but I was having such an enjoyable evening walking with these pretty young girls along the streets of "The Pearl of the Orient" that I decided not to think much about it. Terri had to go home, and all her friends left. Terri said to come to see her tomorrow at work for lunch with just the two of us.

I stopped in a bar close to my hotel to have a Bloody Mary and to think about how I would spend the remaining days of my leave time. I had not seen any of the surrounding areas outside the center of the city and wanted to do that since I did not know if I would ever be back here again. I would ask Terri about that tomorrow. An American soldier in a bar in a foreign city, especially if he is alone, is very popular. Several girls asked if I would buy them a drink, which I did, but I told them that I was not interested in anything else. As I walked back to the hotel, some girls on the street also invited me to spend time with them, which I declined. I went to sleep very happy thinking about Terri and the novelty of this evening and anticipating that in the morning, I would see my new tailor-made suit. The next morning, I went by the tailor's office, and he fitted the new suit on me, measuring and tucking and pinning all the seams and cuffs and collars. It seemed like a very professional operation, and it was fun to be treated like an important person for an hour. When he was satisfied, he said to come back tomorrow, and he would have the remaining details finished and ready for the final fitting.

Then I went to the hotel for lunch with Terri. We ate in the hotel coffee shop, and it was very friendly and casual. She said she wanted to take me to a local club that night. Some of her friends had Chinese boyfriends, and several others had met some Americans on leave, and they would all join us. She gave me the address of the club and directions and the time to meet them later that night. I asked what things she liked to do and what I should see in Hong Kong before I had to return to Vietnam. She said she would give me some ideas later and then she had to return to work. I spent the remainder of the afternoon walking around the city center. I am not a shopper, but if I were, this would be paradise. The department stores were sprawling multi-story buildings containing anything a person could want. There were special shops just for gold or silks or diamonds or fashion eyewear, and on every street, there were huge electronic outlets. There was nothing I really needed, though, so I went to the hotel for a short rest and changed clothes and had a drink in the bar before leaving for the club Terri had pointed out. I was still fascinated by the city and walked slowly to the place we were all to meet.

I was a little late in getting to the nightclub, and Terri was standing alone outside, waiting for me. She did not greet me as warmly as I expected. Instead, she said, "You are late. All your American friends are already here, and they went inside the club. Why are you not here on time? "I'm sorry. They are not my friends; I don't even know who they are. You invited them". That was the only thing I could think to say.

"I have been here alone for 10 minutes," she declared.

I could only manage a string of "I'm sorry."

"You left me standing out here like a common street girl."

Again, a string of multiple "I'm sorry "was all I could think to say.

So she smiled a little bit and uncoiled her tense little body and gave me a warm hug and said, "Don't do this to me again." Note to me. Be on time. Actually, be early. So that made things okay for her; now she knew I would be there for a while. Then she took my arm and led me into the night club.

I do not know if what happened next was planned or spontaneous. When we came into the room, all her friends started cheering and applauding us. I don't know why. They pushed us in the middle of a circle, surrounded us, and sang and clapped. We were supposed to dance in the spotlight. It was too much exposure for me initially, and I tried to resist but was sent back to Terri. So, I forced the resistance to disappear and let the moment happen. The closest thing I could compare it to was the first dance of a couple at their wedding.

After the excitement had passed, Terri and I had some time to sit and talk alone for the first time. I learned she lived with her parents in a traditional Asian way and worked in the western world, which was sometimes difficult for her. In the past, she had a regular boyfriend, but not now. She did not want anything serious or to get married until she was older and decided what she wanted to do. She thought American men were good boyfriends but probably not good husbands. She said "I like you very much, but I don't like that you wear sandals. You should get some proper shoes." I told her it was either the sandals or combat boots. Note to me. See the guy tomorrow morning to trace my feet.

She said, "I am glad you came tonight. For a while, I thought you were not coming, and maybe I was too hard on you." We had a few drinks and danced for a while, not talking much, and it got later in the evening, and I was very happy there. While we were dancing, Terri said, "I have to go home tonight. I can go with you to your hotel room for a while if you would like. I am not a cherry girl'. We left without any of her friends coming with us. And that is all I have to say about that. Terri was busy the next few days, so I could not see her then. She said she had the following two days off and would spend them with me and show me all the things around her city I wanted to see. I was sure it would be wonderful days to spend that time with her except for one major detail. My leave was up and I was supposed to return to Vietnam the next day. I was pretty sure that being AWOL, that is "absent without leave," was always a bad thing and probably even worse if it involved being away from a combat zone. For a time, I pretended to deliberate with the decision and weigh all the possible alternatives and consequences, which might be an Article 15 charge or restriction to base or even a court-martial for desertion if I was absent long enough. But I knew I was staying there to be with her. The rest was a mental exercise I used to make it feel like a rational decision.

So we made plans to spend the days and evenings together for the next two days. Those days passed more quickly than I expected. She showed me all the tourist things I had wanted to see. We took the tram up Victoria Peak and rode the ferry to see the floating fishing village and went on a Chinese Junk evening dinner cruise through the harbor with some of her friends. They played mahjong in the club room while I watched all the lights and ships and other people from the decks. I got my new suit and my new shoes. One night we had dinner and a movie. She picked out an American western with cowboys and Indians and the cavalry coming to the rescue. Then it was time for me to go. She stayed with me late in the evening, and then we said our farewells, but neither of us thought it would be for the last time. I went with her to get a taxi to take her home and watched her leave, and then returned to my hotel for the night. In the morning I took a taxi to the airport.

I was anxious about what would happen when I got there since my leave papers had expired and I was AWOL. I went to the reception area and told them I needed a flight back to Vietnam. The enlisted man checking me in looked at my ID and my leave papers and then went to confer with his commanding officer. After a few minutes, he came back and said, "You are on the next plane that will leave in an hour, Captain. Have a good flight, Sir."

There is no doubt that in the military hierarchy, RHIP or "rank has its privileges." I think this was even more true in Vietnam for the physicians in the Medical Corps. If I had been an enlisted man, I would have been sent to the Military Police for investigation. As it was, I returned with no problem. My commanding officer in Company A either didn't know or didn't care that I had overstayed my leave. Welcome back to Chu Lai. In some ways, I was glad to get back to my job and my friends on the base. We took excellent care of the wounded or sick soldiers when they needed us, and even though I missed being with Terri, all of us at Company A Medical Battalion were also like a family. I was in a relatively secure area in a comfortable hut overlooking the South China Sea.

The rocket attacks fired at us from the mountains were frequent but usually ineffective, and we had well-constructed bunkers when needed. We had a very good mess hall, and we found that the mess at the Signal Corp across the road was even better, so we sometimes went there.

Afternoons and evenings were spent in the officers 'club or playing cards or just hanging out together. One frequent description of being in a war zone is long days of boredom interrupted by a few hours of terror. That applied to us. After several months of being in-country, I was able to get a few more days of leave. I had written to Terri, and she was expecting me.

She had taken some time off from work so we could be together. I went to the American Express office to see her. She said, "Hello, I heard you were kissing another girl."

I did not know what she was talking about. How could that even happen? "Yes," she said. "I heard you were kissing a girl on a stage." Then I remembered at one of the USO shows that toured performing in the camps a singer had pulled me out of the audience, with a lot of help from my friends who actually threw me onto the stage, and she had sung a song to me and kissed me a few times. That entire episode had been very embarrassing for me, so Terri did not question me too much. I never found out how she knew about it. We had a great time together for a few days, and on this occasion, I did not overstay my leave. When I returned to my base there had been some changes.

A new physician had been brought to headquarters. He had previously been stationed at the 4th Battalion, 3rd Infantry, one of the Americal Division outlying bases. He had been transferred because it was discovered he had become addicted to narcotics and was using them while on duty. Generally, I do not judge people since I have many faults of my own and am always glad to have mine overlooked.

In this case, however, he was injecting himself with morphine taken from the syrettes used to inject wounded soldiers and replacing it with saltwater. That is what the wounded soldiers were getting instead of pain medicine. That is difficult for a doctor to rationalize and even more so for combat infantry personnel. He was at our facility temporarily waiting for a decision on a possible court-martial. Our commanding officer summoned me to his office and told me I would have to replace this doctor in Company A of the 3rd infantry until a permanent physician could be assigned there.

Specifically, I would have to leave the next day since the unit was being assigned a secret mission. He did not tell me anything else. I wanted to get a few more details, so I asked my hooch maid, the Vietnamese lady from the nearby village that cleaned our quarters, what was happening.

Secret missions are usually only secret from the ones assigned to it. She said the rumor was that we would be going into the Vietnam highlands to support the Army of the Republic of Vietnam, which was invading Laos to interdict the Ho Chi Minh Trail supply line from North Vietnam. But everyone knew the US Army would also be going into Laos for about a month. Some deal had been made with the government of Laos not to file a complaint about this intrusion by the American Army into a non-combatant neighbor country. The Ho Chi Minh trail was a network of roads, dirt paths, and jungle trails that were used to supply the North Vietnam Army in the south with guns, food, ammunition and even some military vehicles. It ran through Laos close to the Vietnam border. It had been in existence since the time of the French occupation, but now was even more important in keeping the NVA operating. Apparently, our secret mission was going to be disrupting this supply line.

There is a story about the Ho Chi Minh trail. Farmer Tran, who lived in North Vietnam, wanted to help in the war but was too old to join the army. So, they gave him an artillery shell and sent him out on the trail to carry the shell to a base in the south. Farmer Tran walked over mountains and through valleys and across rivers. By day he hid in the rain forest to avoid the US bombers dropping explosives and Napalm and Agent Orange. At night he made his way south, protecting his shell against all the elements and any other dangers. He survived on a handful of rice each day and water from the streams.

After a month of arduous travel, he reached the base and gave his shell to the commander. The shell was put into an artillery piece and fired. The commander then said to Farmer

Tran: "Go get another one." Farmer Tran said, "I will be back soon."

I packed my gear, and in the morning a helicopter arrived to carry me from Chu Lai to the headquarters of my new assignment. There I met my new commanding officer and my medic, "Bop." I never found out his real first name. He was a young black man from Philadelphia and had been there long enough to know what was happening. I did not know anyone in this company, so I would have to depend on him for a lot of support.

Our unit would be moving out in a few days, so Bop took me over to the quartermaster office to get equipped for field duty. I was issued a steel helmet, flak jacket, and a .45 caliber pistol since officers would be required to wear a sidearm. I told the supply sergeant I also wanted an M-79 grenade launcher, a box of hand grenades, and an M-16 fully automatic rifle to take with me.

He declined that request since doctors were not usually front-line personnel. He said I did not need them. I protested, saying that I was a Captain in the medical corps and, as such would be a high grade target for the enemy if we got attacked. He relented and let me have one hand grenade, which he said was only for use in severe emergencies and one Claymore mine in case my foxhole was about to get overrun by sappers. I did not know how to use the Claymore, but it came in a box with detailed instructions which I could read later.

I attached my single hand grenade to the front of my flak jacket. In the morning we were taken by Huey helicopters to a base outside Quang Tri and bivouacked in a field for the night. It started raining, and we did not have any tenting, so Bop and I made a cover with our two shelter-half and were miserable and wet all night. We stayed there for two days and then joined with other soldiers for the secret mission.

We walked to an adjacent airfield and were told to wait until the helicopters arrived. There is a lot of waiting in the Army. Bop and I ate some of our C-rations and got further acquainted. Later in the afternoon the fleet of helicopters arrived in waves. The flight commander loaded us on one, and we flew fast and low across the countryside, first over flat rice paddies and in about an hour into the forested hill country and then into mountain terrain. A landing zone had been assigned to us, and the first choppers came into the site with a spiraling flight path directly over the LZ to reduce the chance of receiving fire from the surrounding jungle. The first wave of soldiers jumped from the choppers as they hovered just off the ground.

They immediately spread out in all directions firing M-16's into the bush and thus secured the area. After a short time, the rest of the company landed, and we immediately sought cover until all the choppers had cleared the area as quickly as possible. The Major in charge of our company assigned Bop and me to an area where we started digging our foxhole.

I learned we would usually be in a place for about three to four days and then be moved to another location where we would repeat the process. Bop and I dug out a fairly deep area that was wide enough for us both to sleep in and covered it with some limbs we got from nearby trees. We then put some empty ammo boxes filled with dirt on top, so we were safe from anything except a direct hit from an enemy rocket. Soldiers were sent out on patrols that would survey the surrounding countryside, look for any enemy activity, and report any contact. They might engage the enemy in a firefight then or call for artillery fire to hit the enemy positions. After several days at this location, we had no NVA contact or activity, so we were moved to another area where we repeated this process.

At the next camp we were on top of a ridge that was open red soil, totally denuded of any foliage. I thought this might be the result of a fire but did not see any burn areas. Bop and I dug a new foxhole, but it was not as good as the one we had before. We had an excellent viewpoint in this open location, and when the NVA were sighted in the valley below, we watched the airplanes come over and drop explosive shells, Napalm, and white phosphorus bombs.

We could also hear the incoming shells fired from artillery banks as they passed over us into the combat areas below the ridge. We sent out multiple reconnaissance patrols, but again there was no contact with the NVA in our immediate sector. So far, my only job was the treatment of minor camp injuries and illness. I had Bop take care of most of them since he was very capable. We were moved again to an encampment to join forces with the cavalry. They were in a sector that had already seen extensive contact with well-armed and effective NVA fighters. Bop and I were assigned an area on the perimeter of the site that already had a good foxhole dug by the previous troops stationed there. We improved the location with an extra layer of ammo boxes and added sandbags around the sides.

Even as we were getting in place, we began getting sporadic incoming fire from the jungle surrounding our position, but we felt relatively secure. One good thing about traveling with the calvary is having a tank with a .50 caliber machine gun and a cannon sitting next to your foxhole. It lets you sleep a little more soundly at night. Patrols were sent out and reported heavy contact with the NVA.

The number of our company wounded and killed continued to climb each day. Most of the badly injured were directly transported by choppers to area hospitals. Bop and I were able to treat many of the minor wounded on-site and keep them in service in the field. I had a difficult decision one morning. A new private, young and obviously shaken, came to me before his platoon was supposed to go on a patrol mission in the bush. He said he had a bad headache and could not go that morning. I examined him as best as possible under the immediate conditions and could find no acute problem, so I sent him back to duty. He refused to go, saying he could not do it. I could not be certain how much he was suffering from real physical pain or fear and combat stress. I again ordered him back to his unit. He still refused. I took him to the commanding officer's tent and reported the situation.

It was not an easy decision. I recommended either he return to duty or face a court-martial for refusing to obey my order to return to combat. The Major agreed and he repeated the order; the infantryman still refused. He was arrested and sent back to the division headquarters. It was a bad decision I made and the results of my not having enough command experience or compassion.

Taking him off patrol for a day and putting him on perimeter guard duty would have given him some time to recover. It would not have damaged discipline in the unit and certainly not have hindered the war effort. I made a mistake that was costly for him. Later I testified at his court-martial that I had certified him fit for duty and he refused to obey. He was convicted and sentenced to a year in a military prison and a dishonorable discharge. It was a harsh sentence for him. The cost of disobedience in the field can be high. I now had some sympathy for such a young, inexperienced soldier.

After the trial, I recommended to the judges they consider reducing his sentence. I never found out what happened to him after that day. It was a lesson for both of us, one I still remember.

On one occasion, I had to be helicoptered to a nearby firebase that had taken a tremendous assault overnight. I arrived early in the morning shortly after the attack was over. Their medic had been wounded, and they had no medical personnel. When I arrived, I treated some of the remaining soldiers for their injuries.

There was one surviving Vietnamese national who was severely wounded and still on the ground. I was not sure if he was an enemy Vietcong or a civilian who had been in the area or both. The company commander wanted to leave him without treatment. He was badly wounded and burned, so I treated him as best I could and insisted that he be sent to a hospital on the next medical helicopter.

After the wounded were treated, I was told to come to the commander's tent. He was a Lt. Colonel and was there with his executive officer. He said he had been wounded by shrapnel during the attack and showed me a little scratch on his arm. I dressed it with antiseptic and a band aid. He then told his aid and me to make sure he was given a Purple Heart citation for his combat injury.

Captains do not get to say no to Lt. Colonels, but I knew absolutely that if those papers came to me for certification, they would be lost in the bureaucratic confusion of war. I was back with my regular unit that afternoon, and we were still receiving a lot of enemy activity. Bop and I took turns standing guard duty at night outside our foxhole on the perimeter of the camp.

We would each do about four to five-hour shifts. My commanding officer said I did not have to stand guard since I was a Captain and he would assign someone to take it, but I actually felt more useful doing it myself. Bop let me use his M-16 rifle when I was there. We made a small bunker behind some sandbags and ammo boxes filled with sand, and we watched from there all night. The jungle was close and full of night noises. I did not know if they were people or animal sounds. Periodically one of the other men on guard duty would shoot up bright flares that lit up the bush for a few minutes, but all it really showed were black shadows and random movement in the bushes. I put my Claymore mine out in front of my bunker. A Claymore is a mine that has two metal plates with a layer of C-4 plastic explosive in the middle. It is fired by an electronic detonator held by the soldier and which is connected to the mine by a long electrical cord.

When detonated by the operator, it throws out a curtain of steel fragments that will obliterate anything within fifty yards in front of it. The army thinks of everything, and on the front of the Claymore, it has specific instructions, so I knew I had it pointed in the right direction. It is used when your position is under attack in close quarters. The Vietnamese used sappers for such an attack.

They are suicide missions in which the attackers would rush into the base perimeter and get as close as they could before throwing grenades they carry in their hands and then exploding their suicide bombs. I was ready with Bop's M-16 and my Claymore and my one emergency hand grenade, but fortunately, they never attacked our base. The following day in the afternoon, the commander came to me and asked me something. One of our patrols had been ambushed in the jungle. They had multiple severe casualties and were still under heavy enemy fire.

They had no medic, and because of the worsening weather and impending darkness and the NVA army surrounding them, the medical evacuation helicopters could not get in to remove them. He wanted to know if I would volunteer to go assist them if he got a team that could get me through the jungle to the place where they were pinned down. He did not specifically order me to go, which he was able to do.

I immediately got my aid kit and a bottle of IV fluids and my combat gear. It was late afternoon when we left. A patrol of about a dozen infantrymen and I began pushing our way through the dense bush and forest. They put me in the middle of the column, which I guess was the safest place to be. The going was very slow since we had to clear a new path to our objective and be totally quiet to avoid being detected. After several hours we reached a small clearing in the jungle where our men were trapped. So far, I had seen no sign of any enemy presence. I checked the wounded men. The sergeant said they had been ambushed and taken some hits, and when they pursued the enemy, they were hit again in a second ambush. I checked one of the soldiers. Part of his skull and brain had been blown off, and death would have been loud and immediate and violent with that type of wound.

He had been placed off to the side of the clearing, and there was nothing to be done for him. The other severely wounded soldier had been shot in the gut. Organs that should have been inside him were lying exposed and mutilated on his abdomen and coved with dirt and burn marks. He had been shot at close range in the second ambush. He was still alive, so no major blood vessels like the aorta had been severed.

His pulse was very weak but palpable; he did not respond to verbal commands but did moan occasionally and had some reaction to physical stimuli. He was still capable of experiencing pain. Doctors cannot always do great things. Sometimes the little things are all you can provide. I had six syrettes of morphine in my medical kit. I gave him three of them.

That was more than enough to ease his suffering and might be considered an overdose. His pulse was so weak I did not know if the drug would even be absorbed enough to reach his brain. Whether I helped or not, it was soon over. The other soldiers had wounds that were severe but not life-threatening, and I could manage them with pressure and dressings. Now we had to get through the rest of the night.

The remains of the original squad and the reinforcements that I came with left us with about twenty soldiers. We were all huddled down in the small clearing in the bush. The night was still overcast with low cloud cover. I could hear the enemy around us, moving in the bush but never saw anyone. There was occasionally rifle fire and explosions in our area, but I could not tell if they were directed at us or not.

Our platoon sergeant called for close-in artillery support, and soon there were massive explosions around us on all sides. Some of the friendly fire shrapnel landed in our cleaning but caused no injuries. After that, all was quiet for several hours. At what I guessed to be close to dawn, I heard movement in the jungle around us, but there was no more gunfire or explosions.

About that time, the medical evacuation choppers came in and were able to hover over the clearing, and we loaded the dead and wounded aboard, and they were gone in just a few minutes. The rest of the night was quiet. Soon the sun was appearing, and we had all survived. I still had my .45

pistol, which I had not even thought about using, and still had my emergency hand grenade fastened to my flak jacket.

We were able to hike to a clearing in the jungle without seeing any enemy soldiers, and in a few hours several choppers were dispatched to pick us up and return us to our base camp. It was a feeling of great relief. Bop was very glad to see me get back. I ate some C-rations for a quick breakfast and took a much-needed rest.

As I lay in my small dark and safe foxhole, I tried to decide how scared I had been in the middle of the night, in the jungle, surrounded by NVA. It is true that you don't think about it consciously at the time, only later. The next day I was sent to another posting that needed medical care. Their medic had been injured and removed from the field. This base was actually larger than the previous ones to which I had been sent and had both cavalry and ARVN components in the area. Except for sporadic sniper fire and occasional rocket attacks, there was not much activity on the first day I arrived. I treated one soldier for gonorrhea.

How, I asked, did you get this infection when we are being shot at every day. He told me that some of the girls from a local village had set up a "steam and cream" shop at a nearby ARVN camp that he visited. So the US Army had a GI Joe grunt stopping to visit local prostitutes and catching VD, and North Vietnam had Farmer Tran who would do everything he could for his country. Was there really any doubt about who would win this war?

The next day we came under heavy rocket attacks from the NVA. One of them exploded close to my foxhole. The blast knocked me down, and I had some minor scrapes and abrasions from flying debris and a slight shoulder separation from the fall. It was not a serious injury and did not prevent me from tending to more severely wounded soldiers. After several days the NVA withdrew their troops, and I was no longer needed and was returned to my previous base. Bop met me when the helicopter dropped me off. He said the company commander had been killed while I was away.

There were a lot of ways to die in Vietnam; combat wounds and tropical infections such as malaria and traffic accidents and friendly fire. The colonel's death was useless. His helicopter was idling on the LZ, waiting for him to board for a recon flight. He approached the craft from the uphill side. Just a brief lapse in concentration, I guess. All Bop could do was put his remains in a body bag. The graves detail would have to sort out the skull and brain from the fragments of his steel helmet and the chopper blade.

In two days, we got the news that our company was being relieved and we would be evacuated to a rear base. Our commander was dead, and forty percent of our soldiers had been killed or had some type of injury. We were no longer effective in the field. The next day I packed up my gear, my grenade, and Claymore mine, and we were transported to Khe Sanh.

Khe Sanh had originally been a military outpost that was the site of one of the largest battles earlier in the war when the US Marines held the base for seventy-seven days' despite being surrounded by a massive opposing force. After they left, the area was filled with land mines and abandoned. Now it had been reopened as a major staging area for this offensive. Bop and I were assigned a real tent. We had a regular field mess instead of C-rations and our first shower in a month. There was a well-equipped field hospital, and I had my shoulder checked. I had x-rays that were all ok, and I just needed my arm strapped down. This base was very secure, and I did not expect to handle any more fatalities here. But there was one more.

One way of clearing the land mines was to suspended a soldier with a mine detector under a helicopter several feet above the ground to locate the devices so they could be exploded in place safely. Bop and I were watching as one such operation took place. The soldier with the mine detector was suspended under a helicopter several hundred feet in the air as he was being transported to another area.

I told Bop I would never be brave enough to do that. I would be afraid of slipping out of the harness. And exactly as I said it, he did. Most deaths in war are loud, sudden, and violent. This one I watched in stop-time slow motion as he tried to climb the air with rhythmic motions of his arms and legs. I was not close enough to hear if he was screaming.

The impact occurred behind a tent close to us, so I did not see him hit the ground. Bop and I ran over to the site. I had not seen any death like this before, and it had not been covered in my medical training manual, so I did not know what to expect. Maybe he would be exploded like a piñata or in fragmented body parts. But when I got there, he was all in one piece, and except for being somewhat compacted and for blood oozing from his nose and ears, there was no great obvious external trauma.

Several other soldiers came over to look at him. One of them said: "those are some nice gloves he is wearing. He won't need them," and he took them off the hands of the dead soldier. I started to intervene by saying we do not strip the bodies of our dead soldiers in arms. I decided not to. I was going back to the rear headquarters and safety, and this young private grunt was heading to the battle zone I was leaving. There was nothing else for me to do, and the graves detail would take over from here.

I went back to our area and later was told the commanding officer wanted to see me. My TDY with the 3rd Infantry was over, and he was arranging for me to be returned to the Americal Headquarters in Chu Lai. He was recommending me for the Bronze Star for my service in combat with his unit and the Purple Heart for my wounds. I thanked him for the honor. Then I remember the Lt. Colonel whom I had treated with a band aid and asked him not to put in the request for the Purple Heart. My small amount of damage was nothing like that suffered by many others in my unit. He agreed with that request. I turned in my combat gear, sidearm and Claymore, none of which I had used.

Bop was the only person I had become friends with on this TDY, so we said our quick good- buys. I gave him my one hand grenade, which I had carried successfully for the past month. I felt like Henry Fleming giving up his badge of courage. A helicopter soon arrived, and I was flown to the airport in Da Nang. I had no written travel orders, and I had been moved around so often in the past month that no one in the military command knew where I was or where I was supposed to be assigned.

There was a daily courier helicopter that flew from Da Nang to Chu Lai on which I could return to my base, but something else entered my mind. It occurred to me that I could possibly take several days and go to Hong Kong before I would be missed. It would involve being AWOL again, but It would not be desertion, which would require a thirty-day absence without the intent to return to duty and would be much more serious. Desertion in time of war could be punishable by death by firing squad. That had only happened to one soldier since the Civil War. Private Edward Slovik was executed for desertion in World War Two despite being given the opportunity to rejoin his unit, which he refused.

It would require some planning, so I went to the base exchange and got some civilian clothes. At the airport, I bought a ticket on a commercial airline to Hong Kong. I was traveling with a military passport and without any leave orders, but nobody questioned me about that. In a few hours I landed in Hong Kong.

I spent three days with Terri and had a great time but was concerned about getting back into Vietnam. I returned on a commercial flight to Da Nang again without any scrutiny. I got on the courier helicopter to Chu Lai and was relieved to know that I was getting back to my duty station without anyone knowing I was AWOL or looking for me. I was quite wrong about that. When I landed, I called my duty station and asked for someone to come pick me up and take me to Company A, Headquarters Division. Very quickly, someone arrived with a jeep and said he was taking me to the Red Cross office instead of headquarters. I did not know what that was about. When we arrived, I went into the office and met the Red Cross agent there. It was very obvious he was under a great deal of stress. After a brief conversation, he was able to tell me they had been looking for me for a week.

He said my father had died of a heart attack, and they had not been able to locate me to let me know. They arranged for me to talk with my family in Ahoskie by telephone. By this time, the funeral service had been finished, and some of the family were just waiting there for me to arrive. There was nothing else to be done now except to arrange for my deployment back to the States.

I met with my commanding officer for the last time. He congratulated me on my service and combat awards and was sorry about the recent death of my father and that I was not able to be located earlier. If he knew I had been AWOL, he said nothing about it. I packed my gear and spent an evening with my friends in the offices club drinking and talking about our time together. We wanted to keep in touch. Mad Dog John and Son of a Bitch Turbovitch had been great friends and support for me the past year. Early the next morning I flew to the main airport near Saigon and had travel orders with a week of travel time to get home. Here are some interesting things about my father. He and I were never particularly close. He was both a victim and a perpetrator of abuse, depression, and alcoholism.

He worked part of his life as a small-town newspaper editor and later as a paper products traveling salesman. Sadly, it was a life of dreams and disappointments. If you knew Willy Loman, then you knew my father. I was sad about his death, but I had not spent much time with him in the past years, and he had not been a major influence in my adult life.

After I reached Saigon, I decided I could not leave without seeing Terri again. I immediately got a civilian flight to Hong Kong. She did not expect me to be back after only a few days away from her, so she knew something was wrong. I explained what had happened and told her that I would be transferred back to the States earlier than I expected. We spent the next three days together all the time. She managed to get off work, and somehow, she arranged to spend the nights with me, which had not happened before. Strangely, it was a time of great happiness and gentle peace for me. We did not do as many things as we usually did on my previous visits. She and I walked around her beautiful Asian city of

Hong Kong and talked about things that were trivial and things important. We spent long nights alone together.

We both knew this might be the end of any relationship we had. One morning I decided I had to return to Saigon and take that flight home to the states. We talked about the future. She said she was planning to move to San Francisco soon and would contact me when she got there. I gave her an address where she could always find me. I packed my suitcase. I put my new tailor-made Hong Kong suit in a storage bag since I did not know when I would wear it again.

I was sure I would open it sometime. Then I was back at the airport on my flight to Vietnam and soon headed back to America. I did not hear from Terri again. No letters ever came. Maybe it ended as it should have. I don't think Rick Blaine expected to get a postcard from Ilsa when she reached America. But it was a time and a memory. If you never experienced a wartime pash, in a city like Hong Kong, with a girl like Terri, then you really missed something.

# Chapter 10

I left Vietnam and after two days and several airplane changes, I landed at Norfolk Airport. The flights were not bad at all. I was traveling in my army khaki uniform and still had my injured shoulder in a sling, so whenever there was an empty seat in first class, I was immediately upgraded. In the airport lounges, my drinks and meals were paid for by strangers who thanked me for my service and asked me about my injuries. I was glad to report they were very slight and thanked them for their support and generosity.

This was a whole new viewpoint for me. A year ago I had been a Vietnam antiwar activist and protesting against that for which I was now being celebrated. I had looked at the returning soldiers as failures or worse, possible war criminals since that story was on the television news every night. The soldiers I had served with were not baby killers or political cannon fodder or sacrificial pawns of US presidents. Like me, they were trying to serve their country as required without doing too much damage to themselves or others and hoping to get back home to their families. Most of us did not agree with the cause for which we were fighting, but felt it was a duty and service required for our country. For most Americans returning from the Vietnam war there were no welcoming ceremonies or parades or celebrations for the soldiers who had lost the war. A single representative from a Veterans group was at the Norfolk airport terminal and met all the returning servicemen with a handshake and welcome home. American boys were still dying in Southeast Asia, and the war was still very unpopular with United States civilians. It would take some time for any healing and empathy and parades and monuments to happen.

My wife met me at the airport. She came alone since that is probably what she wanted. It is about an hour and a half drive to my home in Ahoskie, and we talked about everything that had happened with my father and family. When we got to the house my brothers and sister were there since all of them live near to our home place. My father was not close to any of his three brothers and none of them came to his service. He donated his body to medical science instead of having a traditional funeral, so there was no gravesite to visit. For several years afterward, the hospital that had his remains kept calling us to come to pick up his ashes, and finally, I got them. They were in a small wooden box that spent time on shelves in our various family households. Fifteen years later the box was placed in the corner of my mother's coffin, and they were buried together in the family cemetery plot. That was like a two for one internment. My father would have liked that. He was a very frugal man.

I explained to my family why I was so long in getting back to the states and missed the funeral service. I left out all the details and attributed it to the usual military SNAFU. We are not an emotional family and even on a sad occasion like this, everyone handled grief in a private way. Very soon, things returned to a rather normal state of affairs. I spent some time with Buzzy and his family.

I visited our beach house at Kitty Hawk for a few days. I told my wife that I thought we should get divorced. That was not because I was really expecting anything to happen with anyone else; I knew she was not the person with whom I wanted to spend the rest of my life. She did not want to do it, so I did not pursue it. I still had another year of active duty with the US Army. Since my return from Vietnam was unscheduled, I had not been assigned a new duty station. I contacted the army medical office in Washington to see where they would send me next. Naturally, it was difficult to get any information, so I decided to go there in person. It is not a long drive from Ahoskie up to Washington, and my brother lived in Maryland, so I went there for a few days and met with a representative of the medical corps. I was surprised to learn that since I was returning from a combat zone and had a Bronze Star and Good Conduct Medal, deserved or not, they would try to send me anywhere stateside that I wanted to go for the next year. I had always wanted to learn to snow ski, so I picked Fitzsimons Army Hospital in Aurora, Colorado. I would spend my next year on this base in this suburban city near Denver.

Fitzsimons was an impressive eight-story art deco style hospital on a large medical campus just east of Denver, Colorado. It opened in 1918 as a tuberculosis treatment center for World War One veterans. At its most active time it was the largest military hospital in the country with over 3000 patient beds. It continued to operate during all the US wars, and in the 1970s was a major rehabilitation facility for wounded Vietnam soldiers. I was assigned to the outpatient clinic and emergency department for my tour of duty there. It was an exceptionally easy deployment. In the morning, I would see some active-duty personnel for sick calls and in the afternoons do some routine physicals on retired veterans. About every fifth night, I would cover the small emergency room until midnight. Then I would have the next day off. There was an army residency training program in the hospital, so most of the work was done by the staff and I was primarily a supervisor. The director of the clinic was a very senior Colonel, close to retirement, and was regular army after so many years, but it was still not hard to work with him. I had been promoted to Major by that time, and Majors still did not get to say no to Colonels, but most of the time I was left alone to treat patients.

Beckay and I moved into an apartment complex not far from the base. We had a beautiful view of the Rocky Mountains on clear mornings. The flat plain stretched to the east as far as could be observed. We bought bicycles to ride in the mountains in the spring and summer, and skis for the wintertime. We visited Golden, Colorado, home of the Coors brewing company and Boulder, where the University of Colorado is located. It was nice having a time when very little was required of me and I produced very little in return.

I came late in life to the sport of skiing so I would never become an expert. I had been to the western part of North

Carolina to Boone, which had a few small ski areas and tried it once while I was in college. I fell off the main ski chair lift the first time I attempted to get on it and my instructor sent me back to the bunny hill.

I wiped out on my first downhill run attempt and had a small thumb fracture. One of the people with us injured her leg and we had to take her to the hospital for evaluation. My car slid off a road covered with black ice, and I had to have a tow truck pull me out. The motel we were staying at evicted us for being too noisy. So I was eager to try again with hope for a better outcome.

Colorado, in the early 1970s, became the center of the rapidly growing sport of downhill skiing. John Denver was a local folk singer who gave new meaning to his famous song Rocky Mountain High; a popular sweatshirt recommended people "Ski Stoned."

Aspen was an old Victorian-era mining town rediscovered by the newly rich and famous and where being seen in the latest style fur clothes and boots were as notable as being a top performer on the mountain runs. Spider Sabich, a handsome blond top US professional ski racer, lived in Aspen and epitomized that life of fame, daring, and drugs; sadly, he was fatally shot by his Hollywood girlfriend. She was charged with a misdemeanor gun violation and given a two hundred and fifty dollars fine and thirty days in the county jail, to be served on days convenient to her.

I first learned to ski on child-size three-foot boards in a small resort in Winter Park, Colorado. It was not a spectacular beginning, but over time I became a very good performer and graduated to full adult size equipment. My wife tried it a few times, but it was not a sport in which she developed much interest or skill. I became strong enough to get down any black diamond hill, although not always with grace or form or consistency.

My favorite resort was Snowmass at Aspen, which had an area on top of the mountain called the Big Burn. This had been the site of a forest fire that left the upper reaches open and clear of most of the old trees and was perfect for long fast runs in powder snow. I always tried to be in the first group of people on the lift to reach the fresh untracked new snowfall for the sweetest runs of the day.

The year in Colorado was coming to an end, and I was scheduled to be discharged in the summer of 1972. The US Army asked me to stay on in the service as a career, but I was not interested in doing that. They also said if I stayed as a general medical officer for several years I would be accepted into the Armed Forces Residency Program in dermatology, but that also seemed too far in the future to consider. Strangely, the CIA contacted me and asked if I was interested in working for them. I declined that also. I had no plans for the immediate future and some money saved from my army pay and I decided it was time for an adventure.

All my life I had been supported by other people or educational institutions. This was the first time I was totally on my own. My family had supported me as a child and adolescent. The University of North Carolina had provided me with an education, money, and advisors whenever I needed them. As a medical resident, I had the support of the university hospital and its faculty. After that, I was the property of the US Army. In the summer of 1972 I was honorably discharged and thanked for my service and given my release papers. I decided it was time to revisit my hippie roots for one last celebration of an unencumbered life. I knew that in the near future I would have to get real employment and that if I stayed with Beckay she would want children, and I would probably have to join the Rotary Club somewhere when I settled down in a permanent home.

I found a several years old Dodge van that had been converted to a small camper. It was exactly what I needed. The inside had been modified to have a propane gas stove, an icebox, and a sink with a water supply. There were an L shaped bench and a dining table that could be converted to a bed at night. A pop-up top had been added, so there was standing room inside when it was opened.

The only thing wrong with this van was its uniform white exterior color. We had a send-off event in the parking lot of our apartment complex. The neighbors came over and we had a party with food, music, drinking, and smoking. We painted the outside of the van with rainbows and flowers and sunset vistas and a large green snake that scrolled down one entire side. An alligator was painted on the driver's door and a moonscape on the front. It was a beautiful traveling symbol of the 1970s. The few things we owned were either packed into storage spaces in the van or given to our neighbors, and the apartment was closed. We planned for a six-month road trip. However, the only definite plan was to exit the parking lot of our apartment complex and head north. I was planning to randomly follow the highways of America, as John Steinbeck did with his buddy Charley. And somewhere in that direction was the great state of Alaska and the Alcan Highway.

The road north from Denver runs along the eastern front range of the Rocky Mountains up to Cheyenne, Wyoming. This was an easy country to drive through, and we set our travel pace to be whatever we wanted. Nights could be spent in a campground with showers and a plug-in for electricity and water, or in a primitive national forest with no facilities at all. Each new day could be a driving day, a hiking day, or nothing at all day.

After we stayed a short time in Cheyenne, we headed northwest to Lander, Wyoming. It was not a special town, but I was going there for a special reason. Lander was the hometown of Milan "Son of a Bitch" Turbovitch. His father owned the Lander Bar and Grill, one of many such saloons on the town's main street. I went into his place and sat at the bar with cowboys and Native Americans and miners. I met Mike Turbovitch, owner, barkeep, and Milan's father. Milan and his Australian war bride had moved back to Lander after he left the army. Milan came to meet me at the bar, and we spent the rest of the afternoon and evening remembering old

Vietnam stories and finishing a bottle of Chivas Regal Scotch donated to us by his father. Later I parked the van in his back yard for a few days. It took a full day for me to recover from the hangover.

Afterward, we went hiking and white-water rafting and visiting with his family. When we decided to leave, all of us went to Grand Tetons National Park for a few days of hiking in the beautiful, cool yellow dressed mountains of summer. Then my wife and I left and drove north into Idaho and Montana, going in a general way to Alaska. Milan returned to his home. We kept in touch for awhile by letter. He moved to California and worked in the investment business where he was very successful.

The streams in Idaho were full of large rainbow trout. I caught enough for dinner for several nights. We grilled them on an open fire with potatoes wrapped in tin foil roasting in the coals. Then we went north into Montana and Glacier National Park. This spectacular wilderness preserve, along with its Canadian park neighbor, is over a million acres of lakes, deep valleys, rivers, and snow-topped peaks. It is known as the "Crown of the Continent" and crossed by one of the nation's most famous highways, the "Going to the Sun Road."

We camped in the park and planned a four or five day hike into the backcountry. We packed our tent and camping gear and trail supplies. The walking paths took us through mountain valleys and passes. Some were still covered in snow from the winter storms, and with nature's newest garden of bright yellow glacier lilies emerging from the still white-colored earth.

We shared the footpath with yellow-bellied marmots and ground squirrels and the mountain ridges with bighorn sheep who watched us pass below them. When we were getting our backcountry camping permit, the park ranger advised us about bears. Talking in the abstract about meeting bears in the woods is much different than actually meeting one in the woods.

When you are alone and a big hairy black creature is standing beside the hiking path, seeming to decide whether you are carrying food or are food yourself, it is a different situation. They seem larger in person than in photographs. Back away slowly; don't appear afraid; turn your potable radio up loud and blow your bear horn if you have one. On both of our bear encounters that all worked fine and nothing happened. I don't know if the bears had been conditioned to know how to react with people on the trail, or maybe they were just not interested in us. We camped for several nights in an open meadow by a stream and small lake. For our safety, I suspended our supplies above bear reaching height on a rope tied between two trees and away from our tent.

I usually sleep lightly when camping in the wilderness, partially from altitude sickness, but also because I feel the need to listen for anything that might come around to visit us. The nights stayed peaceful and quiet. The first glow of morning in the eastern sky is always welcomed, as is the first warmth of the morning campfire. Camp days can be spent doing nothing or thinking about doing something or actually doing something. I have tried them all.

After several days we had completed our trek and were back at the campground. This was a full-service facility where hot showers were available and with laundry facilities and a supply store. We spent an extra day here before continuing our trip north. We drove through Alberta to Calgary, which was still very much a cowboy town but missed the annual stampede celebration by a few days. Then we entered the northern Rockies and Banff National Park. This is where I saw my first "real" RCMP officer, complete with squared jaw, red uniform and black boots, and riding a brown horse. I did not know his real name but it could have been Dudley Do-Right of cartoon fame. He may have been real or a colorful backdrop for tourists like us, but I was impressed either way.

We hiked in the mountains. We rode horses up to Lake Louise. It was still mostly undeveloped then. The lake is named for Princess Louise, the fourth daughter of Queen Victoria. It is the perfect deep blue, clear mountain lake and the subject of many artists who painted it as we watched for a while. Occasionally we would leave our camper for a night or two and stay in hotels so we could wash and relax in a more comfortable setting.

The Banff Springs Hotel, a turn of the century luxury hotel was our home for several nights. It opened in 1888 as one of the best lodging places in Canada. I got to enjoy the spa and the gardens and high tea in the afternoon. Then we returned to living in the van and resumed our drive, this time passing through glacier ice fields up to Jasper National Park, an expansive Canadian wilderness area. We camped in the still snow-covered valleys and hiked on glaciers of deep blue ice and kayaked through swift-moving ice-cold streams.

Then we entered British Columbia, Canada, and had a leisurely drive to Dawson Creek, a city with a "mile 0" marker in the center of town. It is the official beginning of the Alcan Highway. There were 1,488 miles of mostly dirt and gravel road to our destination of Fairbanks, Alaska. This is not a Sunday afternoon drive.

The Alcan Highway was built by the government in 1942 to transport men and supplies to military bases that were opening in Alaska at the beginning of World War Two. In the early 1970s, it had not been paved but was still maintained to some extent. The winter snows, floods, and landslides took their toll each year on the fragile narrow passage through the Canadian wilderness.

Winters were usually not passable at all and a trip at any time required extensive preparation. We planned for about a week to make the drive, giving us enough time to see the area and for any unexpected delays we might encounter. The most important requirement was to carry three or four spare tires and the tools to change them. The road was gravel with potholes, and some places were rocky washboard areas that could macerate a tire. Service facilities were many miles apart with little chance of immediate assistance. The front of the vehicle should be covered with wire screening to prevent damage to the radiator and windshield from flying debris and falling rocks. The vehicle should have high clearance and preferably have a skid plate to protect the engine and drive train and fuel tank from damage.

Several extra gas cans should be carried in case the few service facilities were out of fuel. An emergency shortwave radio should be available. The road dust would be so thick that the windows and air vents should be sealed with plastic to keep it out. I bought two extra tires and a better lug wrench and an extra gas can. The rest would have to depend on good fortune.

The paved road was soon behind us. The highway goes through broad open plains and long mountain valleys carved by glaciers; over high passes and around streams and lakes. The scenery is dramatic in all directions. Wildlife is frequently present in all these areas and sometimes on the road. Most of the time, we were the only vehicle on the highway. Occasionally we would meet a large transport truck coming the other way. It would be visible as a moving cloud of dust before you could see the truck itself. After a few rock pits in the windshield, I learned to pull over and avoid the shower of gravel they created. You know you are becoming used to the drive when a moose on the road causes you to start blowing your horn instead of stopping to take another moose picture. Except for one flat tire, the first few days were uneventful.

We camped by a lake one night and at a rest stop on another. There were small service stations at intervals along the highway, where we bought gas and supplies as needed. I stopped talking about the high price of everything. I wondered what the people who ran these stops were like. The places were usually makeshift stations and garages. They could repair almost anything.

The homes they lived in were small houses or trailers. I asked one owner if he stayed there all year. He said he liked the solitude in the winter even better. The next day we picked up a hitchhiker on the highway. I did not know how or why he was there, but it was the 70s, and people, in the spirit of Jack Kerouac, were "on the road," trying to find themselves. He was a young guy, appeared to have no supplies, and was hungry, so we gave him some sandwiches. He rode with us for a day, and we let him off in Whitehorse, the only large town in the area. The following day we met two young girls who were backpacking for the summer. They rode with us for two days. We left the Alaskan Highway and took the Klondike Highway to Dawson City in the Yukon Territory.

It was about gold. For five thousand years, gold has been the creator and destroyer of boomtowns and trading meccas; of empires and rulers of empires; of a few who struck it rich and more who went busted or became widows and orphans. Gold covered the sarcophagus of ancient Egyptians and the crowns of modern-day kings and queens.

I have seen it adorning beautiful women, hanging like golden icicles in the shop windows of the Middle Eastern souks, and in South American Inca displays where it was plentiful enough to use for cups and plates. And now I could see a few flecks of the bright yellow metal at the bottom of my gold pan. It is called "gold fever." This element was created in the fiery death of an exploding star, thrown into space and then coalesced as part of a new rocky planet 4.5 billion years ago; then cooled and solidified in the rocks and soil of this newly formed Earth.

Now, washed by time and rain and erosion into Bonanza Creek, a tributary of the Yukon River, it was in my gold pan and belonged to me. All the known gold in the world would fit in a cube twenty meters on each side. I had prospected a small amount of it, and now it belonged to me.

I had bought my gold pan and the permission to prospect for a day at the same gold claim site where George Carmack, on August 16, 1896, discover giant gold nuggets and started the great Yukon gold rush. By 1897 the news had spread throughout the United States, and the exodus to Alaska reached its peak. One hundred thousand dreamers headed for the goldfields.

Maybe forty thousand reached them. Some were discouraged by the difficulty and expense of the undertaking. Some died in the snow and the cold and the avalanches on the Chilkoot Pass and the White Pass that had to be crossed to reach Dawson City. Accidents killed some, and fights over gold claims killed others. Some died in the general frantic activity of a boomtown that grew from a few thousand to over thirty thousand people in a year. Most did not get rich prospecting for gold. In just a few years all the easy pickings were gone, and then all the miners were gone too. Gold fever had come and gone in the Yukon Territory. Coincidently, we arrived in Dawson City on Discovery Day, August 16. 1972. This anniversary was celebrated each year as a regional holiday.

For a week the town was recreated in the style and spirit of 1896. There was a parking lot for campers in the center of town, and we stayed there for several days.

I spent one afternoon in a frontier bar, drinking with an elderly lady dressed in the old camp style. She had a gold nugget the size of a small fist tied around her neck with a piece of knotted cotton cord. I bought her a drink and asked her if that was real. She said: "Sonny, it sure is." I asked her if it was safe for her to walk around like that with it only secured with a piece of old rope.

She said everyone knew her, and no one would bother her. The things you hear day drinking in a bar may not be true, but I said I believed her. I walked a few blocks to the edge of town were Jack London's cabin was located. He was one who had heard the "call of the wild" and came to the Yukon to answer that call and write about it. Robert Service worked there as a banker and composed in his verse the mixture of tragedy and humor found in the hard life of prospectors living in the spell of the gold rush. I hiked up a trail along the river to a played-out mining claim. I found the crumbling remains of a wooden sluice box and the foundation of a small cabin. Everything is protected as a historical landmark, and nothing is supposed to be disturbed. I found a rusty harmonica partially buried in the dirt. It looked pretty old, and I wondered if it had belonged to one of those miners who may have played it on those long cold nights; more likely, it had been lost recently by a tourist, but I decided to keep it anyway. At night there were celebrations and parties in the old buildings. I met Pierre Berton, who had written a history of the era in a book, "Klondike," and he autographed a copy for me.

In the Grand Palace Dance Hall, an original building still standing from the stampede days, there was a show with can-can dancing girls and music from the gold rush era. With some imagination and a few hours of partying, it was possible to be back in that time for a while. The next morning it was time for us to leave. I carefully packed the small bottle of gold I had panned and my gold pan in case I came across a site that looked like it could be the beginning of a new gold rush. I still had a touch of gold fever.

The final portion of the road from Dawson City to Fairbanks was the most rugged and lightly traveled part of the highway system. Parts of the road were little more than narrow gravel paths through valleys and mountain passes. It is a four-hundred-mile trip with few services available. We were about halfway through this segment when we rounded a bend in the road, and a gang of people jumped from the side of the road and surrounded our van, forcing us to stop.

I grabbed my pistol in alarm but then saw it was a family; a father, wife, and several kids who had stopped us. There was a station wagon parked on the side of the road. It looked like we had been ambushed by the Brady Bunch.

They said they had been driving from Fairbanks and had been stranded there all day with two flat tires. We were the only car to come by. They had followed this road on their map but were not equipped for this type of driving. I remembered we had passed a service station about forty miles behind us. In this situation, I could see that assisting others was imperative.

My wife stayed there with the family, and I took the father back to the station to get his two flat tires repaired. Then we returned to the station wagon and got the tires changed so they could finish their trip. He bought me a tank of gas for my time and trouble. We spent one more night camping along this road, and the following day, we reached Fairbanks, Alaska, the end of our driving for now.

## DR. GEORGE T. GRIGSBY AND DR. LUCIUS BLANCHARD

# Chapter 11

Fairbanks was the northernmost place I could drive on the Alaskan highways. We rested there for a few days and saw the local sites. I talked to some of the long-time residents who told me that if I was there in the winter, and went outdoors without proper protection, I could freeze to death in thirty minutes. I learned that information while sitting in the Malamute Saloon, a local bar rebuilt from the original days of the town. We spent a night there drinking and listing to a recitation of the poems of Robert Service.

But there was still a destination I desired farther north. On the map, it is about 66 degrees, 33 minutes, and 48 seconds above the equator. In this place there is at least one day in the summer where the sun never sets below the horizon and one day in the winter when the sun never rises above the horizon. It is any place above the Arctic Circle.

I found there was a town named Kotzebue just north of the circle, and we were able to get a flight there to spend a night in the community. It was primarily a Native American settlement of about 1500 people, a regional center for trading and commerce, and a gateway city to the arctic.

The small plane landed very near the town. It was close to lunch when we arrived, and when I got off the flight, I saw I could get Kentucky Fried Chicken from Colonel Sanders dressed in a fur parka. I chose that over dried salmon, seal cakes, or whale blubber, which seemed to be the other choices in town. The rest of the day was spent watching and learning about local Inuit and Native American activities. I had hoped to see the northern lights, but they did not appear. The next day we were back in Fairbanks where we bought new tires and resupplied the little van as we prepared to head south to Mount McKinley.

In 1975 the local name of the park and mountain was changed to Denali, and after some partisan political fighting, the US Government accepted this as the official name of the park. The mountain is the tallest in North America at 20,310 feet. We camped here for several days. In the summer the sun does not set until about eleven pm and rises a few hours later. The night sky is never very dark. There are many grizzly bears in the park and we decided not to hike here. I did not think a portable radio and a bear horn would make much difference to a 750-pound top predator.

Many bears were visible from the road and viewing sites, which was close enough. The park was one of the few areas where Arctic wolves were still present. The park ranger said they were not seen often, but occasionally they would come at night to a small lake near the campground. I set up a makeshift camp blind in the area and waited at night to see if any would come; none did.

After a few days here, we continued south to Anchorage and camped there for a few nights. I decided there was one more prominent place I wanted to visit and take my new gold pan. Nome, Alaska is famous for the last big American gold rush in 1899 and memorialized in stories and song and film and on the stage.

They say the gold deposits in Nome were so rich it could be scooped up on the beach and carried out in sacks. There was no need to even mine for it. As in all the previous booms, it was soon over. The days I spent with my pan on the Nome beaches produced nothing of any value, and eventually my enthusiasm faded along with my dream of sudden riches. I packed away my gold pan for good. I met the Alaskan bush pilot who flew the mail plane to the isolated villages along the coast, and he let me fly with him to White Mountain to help deliver the mail. While we were on the ground, I watched the natives skin a seal they had caught, and I visited the neighborhood health center. When they found out I was a doctor, the nurse had me check a few patients that were there for simple problems. Later back in Nome, I met an undertaker in a bar one afternoon who told me that when people in Nome died in the winter, they could not bury them until summer because the ground was too frozen. I thought that sounded unlikely. There is a lot of questionable information to be learned from day drinking in local bars.

The early autumn nights were starting to get longer and cooler, and it was time to head south. From Anchorage, we went to the town of Homer, on the Homer Spit, a finger of land extending from the Kenai Peninsula and nicknamed the "end of the road." It is an area known for fishing and crabbing. I rented a crab net for a day and caught a large number of Dungeness crab from one of the fishing piers in the city. I traded them at a local processing plant for some cleaned crab meat and fixed crab salad for dinner one night. On Homer Spit, there is a bar favored among locals called the Salty Dog Saloon, and we spent several nights eating and drinking there. A salty dog is still one of my favorite drinks. We continued south to Skagway and took the narrow-gauge railroad over White Pass to Haines, Alaska. This is a terminal for the ferry that takes people on the inside passage along the coast to the continental United States port in Bellingham, Washington. We bought a ticket for the whole journey, but it was possible to get off anywhere the ferry stopped and then board the next scheduled ferry in a few days to continue the trip without any additional cost. We could sleep in the van on the lower vehicle decks on the overnight runs, but most people camped out on the upper open decks, so we joined them.

This was a gathering of whoever you could think of moving together. There were travelers like us, loggers and fishermen, seasonal workers leaving before the winter arrived, a few workers from the beginning of the pipeline construction, and wanderers. They were willing to share their music and beer and drugs and stories. I was not expecting a "happening" on the upper deck of an Alaskan ferry, but there it was. We stopped at Juneau to see the state Capital and at Kodiak for the Russian churches. A Russian Orthodox Priest we met in his cemetery gave us a tour of his small church. We saw the totems in Ketchikan. After a week, we disembarked in

Bellingham. Five months earlier, we had left Denver with no definite itinerary. Now it was time to head east and home for a short while and then plan something for the future. We drove along the Oregon coast and Big Sur California, then through Los Angeles and San Diego and down to Tijuana. From there, we went through the American southwest, to the Grand Canyon for a day hike and then up to Mesa Verde National Park in Colorado where we camped. Since it was the beginning of winter there were few people in the park, and that night there was a storm that left a foot of snow on the ground.

The only other campers there were a young couple who were sleeping in a little tent down the road from us. We were snowed in for a while so, I invited them over to the van to get warm and have breakfast. Later in the day, a ranger arrived with a snowplow, and we were able to continue our trip home. By the time we reached St Louis, the gas, supplies, and my cash reserves were getting low. I stopped at a filling station and traded one of the extra tires I no longer needed for a tank of gas and then continued on through Kentucky and Virginia for our last day of travel.

It was now early December, and my wife and I were back in Ahoskie. I had called my family occasionally while we were on the road, so they were expecting us and glad to see us after our being away with little contact. I knew I could not stay here for a long time, but it was good to have a home base for a while and get acquainted with my brothers and sister and their families and to see Buzzy again.

Beckay and I drove down to her home in South Carolina to see her family. I am not their favorite relative-in-law, but the visit was fun for a few days. I told Beckay that I thought we should get separated for a while and see how that worked. I still knew she was not the person I wanted to be with forever, but she said she was not ready for that. She wanted to keep trying to make it work.

It was time for me to find a job somewhere and make some money. I had a medical license in North Carolina, so I looked at opportunities in that area. In the first part of January I started work as a physician in the emergency department at Cape Fear Valley Hospital in Fayetteville, NC. It was a very busy place, and I had to take on a lot of responsibility for critically ill or injured patients since it was the largest hospital in the area.

It was also close to Ft. Bragg, home of the 82nd Airborne Division, reported to be the best light infantry force in the US Army and able to be deployed anywhere in the world in eighteen hours. Fayetteville was a community of family farms and old southern tradition mixed with all the newly arrived camp-followers that are found wherever large military installations are built.

I soon learned the director of the emergency department was a partially reformed alcoholic general physician and that I would be undertaking more responsibility than I had originally anticipated, but I knew this was a short-term arrangement, so I decided to stay.

The medical experience I had in Vietnam was invaluable since the area was noted for the regular Saturday night meetings of the local knife and gun clubs, with their subsequent injuries and even occasional fatalities. We had our regular occurrences of myocardial infarctions, strokes, accidents, and drug overdoses. Most of these I was able to treat successfully in our facility. Some of the difficult or serious cases would be referred to the UNC hospital in Chapel Hill.

I knew I would not be here for a long time and would soon start looking for another residency program to finish my training, and I was still thinking seriously about dermatology as an attractive specialty. After working for a year, I began applying to dermatology training programs. Currently, that is the most desired medical specialty and only available to the very best students. There are fifty applicants for each training position, and only the top students have any chance to be selected.

When I started looking at residency programs, the process was very informal. There was no established dermatology match program. I filled out applications and was usually invited for an interview. If the applicant and the program training director though it would be a good fit and they had an open training slot, they could offer you a position at that time. I applied and interviewed at some of the best programs in the country, including the Mayo Clinic and the Medical College of Georgia, and was offered positions at some of them. I did not get admitted to the University of North Carolina, although they said they would consider me in the future when they had an open training position.

As part of my application process, I had to get letters of recommendation from the directors of my previous internal medicine residency training program. I contacted them at the

Medical College of Georgia with my request for them to provide one. A few days later, I received a phone call from the doctor who had been head of the internal medicine department while I was there. He said he and several of his staff were moving to become head of the University of Louisville School of Medicine.

He said they remembered me from three years ago as an outstanding resident, and asked if I would consider coming to Louisville for a year as their Chief Medical Resident. I would be in charge of about thirty residents, interns, and all the medical students when they rotated through our service. I don't know if they really thought I was good or just could not find anyone else available at the time, but it sounded like an excellent opportunity for me.

I sent an application to the dermatology department at the University of Louisville and scheduled an interview with them. When I went to interview in the internal medicine department, they told me the position of Chief Resident was mine if I wanted it. The next day I was interviewed by the head of dermatology. They had my application. I told them I would be the Chief Medical Resident there this year, and after that was over, I would like a training position as a dermatology resident. They said okay. It was the shortest interview I have ever had. The DMV asks more questions and takes longer to make a decision than they did. Again, I did not know if it was on merit, or they just needed someone to fill the spot, but I accepted both positions.

The Chief Residents' job is primarily administrative with the supervision of the medical house staff and with some medical teaching. It is between being a house officer and junior faculty. In some respects, it can be considered an unproductive year unless the doctor is staying in academic medicine or in a career in medical education or administration. After finishing their basic internal medicine residency, most doctors will go into private practice or have additional training in one of the medical subspecialties. For me, this was the perfect situation. I had been out of the university education environment for three years. The job I was taking was not particularly difficult, and dermatology training would follow. I know I would be getting exactly what I had hoped for. Once again, I had been very lucky.

I resigned from the position in the emergency department at Cape Fear Valley Hospital. The physician in charge there tried to bribe me to stay longer, without success. I could see his personal problems would soon end his usefulness to the hospital, and I did not want to be involved in any future there. The few things we owned were packed in a U-Haul rental truck, and in the summer of 1974, we moved to Louisville, Kentucky.

# Chapter 12

General Hospital in Louisville was different than the places in which I had worked before. It was the central public hospital in a big Midwestern city and open to anyone who needed medical care. We had general outpatient clinics, specialty clinics, and large in-patient wards where both complicated and routine medical patients could be treated.

It was in a downtown central medical complex of multiple hospitals, including Jewish Hospital, the Methodist Hospital, and Norton Children's Hospital. These were for private and well-insured patients. In the General Hospital, the resident staff was given a lot of responsibility for the medical care of patients, so it was an excellent hands-on opportunity to learn.

I had a small office in the administration area. It was adjacent to the office of the Chief of Medicine. The staff of medical residents was a mixture of graduates of the Louisville School of Medicine, some foreign medical graduates, and a few from other training programs. The residency program here was not yet in the top tier of training positions since it was being rebuilt with new teaching staff, and the physical plant was dated. The original General Hospital was built in 1823 and then replaced by the newer facility we were in, which opened in 1914. The complex was a group of buildings adapted for various purposes over the years. They had been renovated and modernized multiple times for multiple uses. It showed its age and needed total replacement.

The main in-patient facility still had large open wards with many beds separated only by curtains which could be opened or closed to give a small amount of privacy for the patients who occupied the beds. It was like a scene from M*A*S*H, where the doctors and nurses and staff walk from bed to bed, talking about the patients as they move along.

My job included running the morning report each day. Residents would present a synopsis of the new patients they had admitted and review their initial findings with the attending physician and me. It could be stressful since it was expected that the resident would present adequately examined patients with the appropriate treatment underway. Another very enjoyable part of the work was running the Grand Rounds each week.

This is when all the staff, residents, and students come together to discuss an interesting case with specialists from different fields. I would meet with department heads and get them to present cases they might have. I was the first Chief Resident to ask the dermatology department to present a case at grand rounds. It was a patient with severe erythema multiforme, a life-threatening skin disease.

I made ward rounds with one of the medical teams each day and sometimes substituted for the attending physicians if they had to be away. I handled all the daily administrative details of the interns, residents, and medical students in our department.

Cases on the large wards could be of any level of complexity. On one ward we had a young man admitted with a moderate case of gastroenteritis and dehydration. He was put in one of the beds to receive IV fluids and monitoring of the electrolytes in his blood. There were multiple severely ill patients in the same ward, and that afternoon there were two "code blue" incidents, which are cardiac arrests. Neither of the patients could be resuscitated, and they were carried out under white sheets through the ward passageways on a gurney. The young man went to the nurses' station and asked if he could call his wife. He told his wife," You have to come to get me out of here, they're dropping like flies!" I don't know if she came to get him or not.

When I finished my year in the medicine department, they presented me with an official U of L engraved staff chair which I still use. I took and passed the Internal Medicine Board Exam on the first attempt, which at that time was unusual. Again, lucky guessing for me. Then I walked down two long corridors to a small group of rooms in the back of the medical complex. This would be my home in dermatology for the next two and a half years.

Training in dermatology is acquiring a mixture of skills in the medical treatment of illness, pathology, and surgery. We were fortunate to have teachers who were adept in all these areas. This was also a very low-pressure learning environment. We all had a good time working together. Pat and Mike and I were the three first-year residents. There were seven residents in the second and third-year training slots. Some of our education took place in the private offices of the faculty, which were near the main hospital and in the hospital clinics where the residents were usually in charge. There was some supervision by volunteer dermatologists in private practice in the community. We had some unusual situations in our department. It was not highly structured and open for a lot of independent learning. Our Chief of Dermatology was quite advanced in age and past his prime years in practice but not yet willing to retire. He was chief in name only, and the department was run by other faculty members.

One of the jobs of the senior residents was to be with the chief when he was seeing patients to ensure nothing went badly wrong. One day I was with him when he wanted to remove some small flat warts on the face of a young man by using a soldering iron to burn them out. I convinced him to use a less scarring method to do that. He did retire while I was there and was remembered with great respect for a long and distinguished career that ended well.

In our second year of training, we spent four months assigned full time to the plastic surgery department. Some of the residents thought this a waste of time and were only observers. For me, it was an excellent opportunity to improve my surgical technique. I had years of experience in basic surgery skills in the army and emergency room work, so I was more comfortable in this setting than the other residents who were just out of medical school. As is frequently the case, the head of plastic surgery was a prima donna, with a giant ego, but after some time he did learn to tolerate me. Sometimes, I would take first call when the plastic residents were busy, and he let me do some simpler cases in the operating room by myself when the other residents were occupied with major procedures. I knew I had been marginally accepted by him when he started including me in his frequent doctor rants about how he had to put up with his plastic surgery residents and this "dermatologist who thinks he is a plastic surgeon."

The new head of the dermatology service was only about ten years older than I and a very interesting person. He was skilled in his profession and successful in business. He owned a number of apartments and office buildings in town. He was very relaxed and had a good sense of humor. He and a group of his residents were permanently barred from the Playboy Club in Chicago for excessive rowdiness. I was with him at the time; I was not loud but got expelled anyway. He was not as successful in relationships and had several ex-wives in his history. He once initiated a gunfight with a plastic surgeon over a woman. He explained later that it was just a friendly misunderstanding. He only winged him and so spent several months doing easy time in prison. I helped cover his patients while he was away. He was an accomplished person in many ways, and I liked him very much as a teacher and later in our careers as a friend.

Becky and I lived in a small house in a Louisville suburb. It was actually one of the favorite places I have owned. It was at the end of a small street and had a garden in the back where I could grow various kinds of vegetables and plants. When we decided to move to Louisville, I again discussed a trial separation, but she said no. Instead, we went into couples counseling and had a baby. His name is Hayes.

Since I was board certified in internal medicine, I was given six months of training credit for that time and finished my dermatology residency early. I had still not made any definite plans about what I would do next. I had been reading about a new type of surgery that was being introduced into the dermatology field by Doctor Fredrick Mohs at the University of Wisconsin. It was a way of treating large and difficult skin cancer using a new skin mapping technique to track the tumor spread. It gave a much higher rate of cure than other types of surgery being done by plastic or conventional surgical procedures. Nobody in Louisville was trained in this or even knew too much about it. It sounded interesting, like something I would like to know about. I learned there were very few places that taught this technique, and only a few people a year could be trained in it. I decided I would look into it more seriously.

I called Dr. Mohs at the University of Wisconsin in Madison. I was surprised he took my call, and he was very cordial. I asked about doing a fellowship with him and learning Mohs surgery. He said he would consider it, but there was a five-year waiting list to get a training position with him. I thought that it was too long for me to wait, so I asked if I could come to watch him for a few weeks and see what it was about and make a decision later.

He was fine with that and said I could come whenever I wanted. Later I found out this was a very common request and that people were visiting him from all over the world to see what he was doing. He was also getting patients from throughout the United States referred to him as well as some who were coming from foreign countries for treatment in his clinic.

I took a flight to Madison and checked into the YMCA, which was close to the University of Wisconsin Medical

Center. Then I went to see Dr. Mohs at his clinic. There were visitors from several other schools there. His current fellow, who was from Amarillo, Texas, was finishing his training. A new fellow had just arrived from Duke University to start his training with Dr. Mohs. I spent the next week watching them work.

Mohs surgery is not for the timid physician. The tumors he treated were the most advanced and horrific cancers that had recurred after multiple previous treatments had failed. Dr. Mohs used a technique in which the tumors were coated with a caustic paste that killed the tumor and surrounding skin. Each day a layer of dead skin and cancer tissue would be removed and checked to see which way the cancer had spread.

Another layer of skin would then be removed in that area. Large tumors might require multiple days of treatment to achieve the eradication of all cancer cells. In the process, entire noses, ears, and large portions of the face might have to be removed. Open areas down to the bone would take months to heal. On a few occasions, cancer had spread into the eye sockets, and the eye had to be removed. Some cases required removal of bones of the face and skull. All this is done while the patient is awake. Mohs surgery is not for the timid physician; after the first week the doctor who had just arrived from Duke to take the fellowship training position quit. He said it was not something he could do and was gone the next day. It is the only time in history that anyone has left a Mohs training position.

Even though I had only been in the clinic for a few weeks, Dr. Mohs did know who I was. I was just an observer, but had managed to help in a few non-surgical areas, such as preparing specimens and examining the microscopic slides with him. I immediately told Dr. Mohs that I could stay for the entire training period and take over the fellowship position. He said he would think about it, but added that he had a list of a dozen or more doctors who had been waiting for years to come train with him.

I did not know if impersonating a licensed physician would be a misdemeanor or a felony under the Wisconsin legal code. I had no Wisconsin medical license or affiliation with the University of Wisconsin Medical Center at all. I was just a visiting doctor standing there watching. Despite this, I put on a white coat and found the hospital ward where Dr. Mohs patients were admitted. I told the nursing staff I was his new assistant and gave them my name and phone number and said to call me if any patients needed anything at any time. Security and physician verification were very lax, so no one asked me for any identification.

I was at the clinic door every morning before Dr. Mohs got there and made sure I never left before he did. Fortunately, one night a patient had some mild post-op bleeding, and the nurses in the ward called me. I came over to the hospital and took care of the patient. They did not have to call Dr. Mohs. The next day he read in the patient's chart that I had covered the emergency for him.

Dr. Mohs was a big gruff-seeming German physician who talked very little. He expected his staff and employees to be loyal and competent. He operated in his own designated clinic that he controlled somehow independently of the university and could do whatever he wanted. He was not a dermatologist, as many people thought. He was a general surgeon but spent most of his time with dermatologists. The following day he said I could stay for the fellowship. I do not know if that happened because of my persistence, or maybe nobody else could come at that immediate time. I did not care either way. I had been standing around with no definite plans and had fallen into the most sought after skin cancer fellowship in the country and with the most renowned skin cancer surgeon in the world—another very lucky day for me.

I moved from the YMCA to an apartment close to the Medical Center. Beckay and Hayes had been staying in Louisville and moved to Madison to be with me. The work was long hours and stressful days but also very rewarding. I loved it. We did surgery six days a week, and on Sundays we would do research and write medical papers about the new advances we were making.

I did not see much of Madison except for my apartment and the Medical Center and the road between them. My only other lasting memory of the area was how cold it was and wondering why anyone would live here. It was a place in which I would never consider living permanently.

Beckay and I decided it was time for us to separate for a while. Neither of us were happy in our situation. I would stay in Madison to finish my fellowship, and she and Hayes would return to Columbia, where she would get a job teaching and live with the aunts who raised her when she was a child. This was difficult for both of us since there was now a son involved. Before she left, we discussed that we would see how things worked out, and we might get back together again after I left Madison. Because we had Hayes, we would have a working relationship for the next eighteen years but would never live together again.

As I neared the end of my fellowship, it was time to decide where I would go to practice dermatology and Mohs Surgery. I was about the twenty-fifth person in the world to be trained in this field. I was also board certified in both dermatology and in internal medicine. Additionally, I was a Vietnam Veteran with a not entirely deserved honorable discharge. Because of all these things, there were many opportunities available to me. I remembered meeting a dermatologist the prior year at a conference who said I should talk to him about a job when I finished my training. He seemed like a nice guy, and he lived somewhere very warm.

# Chapter 13

"No, we have houses just like any other city," replied Dr. Harold Boyer when I asked him if I would have to live in a hotel if I moved to Las Vegas. I was a senior dermatology resident and attending a conference in Aspen, Colorado. In the morning session I was sitting beside a dermatologist from Las Vegas.

He was older and quite friendly. After some minutes of conversation, he said I should think about Las Vegas as a place to practice. He was looking for some younger doctors to join him. At present, he had an elderly partner, Dr. Primo Mori, who had retired from his practice in Pennsylvania and moved to Vegas and was working part-time

He said Las Vegas was a great place to live. There were about 300,000 people in the valley, the weather stays nice all year, and there were always interesting things to do. The economy was strong and people were looking for places to retire in the southwest, so the city was expected to grow even larger in the future. I said that sounded okay, but I was not really a gambler and preferred outdoor recreation instead. He said Las Vegas had all that too.

There was great hiking and climbing in the Spring Mountains thirty minutes away from the city. Mountain Charleston was forty-five minutes away, almost 12,000 feet high, and had a ski area. Thirty minutes from the city, there was Hoover Dam and behind it Lake Mead, the largest man-made reservoir in the United States. Southern Utah and Zion park, the Grand Canyon, and Death Valley were all only a few hours' drive. He said to call him if I had any interest in joining his practice.

My only previous exposure to Nevada and Las Vegas was driving through on a trip to California and stopping to eat and playing a slot machine in one of the casinos. So my recalled image of the place was a hot, dry desert and lots of hotels along the Strip; and the fifty dollars I did not have anymore. So, I did not give it any serious consideration at the time. Nonetheless, I did remember his name as something that might come up in the future.

In the fall of 1978, I finished my fellowship in Mohs surgery and had to decide where I should go to practice. Dr. Mohs suggested I could stay there and work with him, but the weather in Madison was not attractive to a southern native. There were very few doctors in the United States trained in Mohs surgery, and we had a map of where each of them was in practice. I studied the map and there was no one doing this surgery in the entire state of Nevada. I remembered my conversation earlier with Dr. Boyer. I had lived in various areas of the United States during my medical training and army career but never in the southwest, so I decided I could go there for a year or two until I chose a permanent home, which I expected to be in the southern states.

I called Dr. Boyer and said I had decided to work with him. Of course, he did not really remember me, but he said that was fine, and I should come for a visit to get reacquainted, and he would help arrange for me to start working there.

Las Vegas, in those days, still had the reputation of being the wild, wild West. My friends and fellow residents usually had a surprised look on their faces when I told them where I was going to work. I was a little surprised myself when I realized I was actually moving to Las Vegas, also frequently known as Sin City and Lost Wages. It was a time when organized crime, good old boy politicians, shady business operators, and people who had failed elsewhere could become successful in Nevada. Getting a license to practice medicine was easy. I filled out a few forms and sent in copies of my training certificates and went for a ten-minute interview. When the licensing committee found out I was joining Dr. Boyer, they had no other questions.

Many doctors who came to Nevada were very good. Some had lost their license to work in other states. I met some who were licensed but seemed to have almost no formal training at all. Nevada was still at that time, the last frontier in many ways.

Dr. Boyer arrived in Las Vegas by accident. In 1952 he was finishing his residency in Oklahoma and was taking a train to California for a job interview. The train had a stopover in Las Vegas, and Dr. Boyer went to visit the only dermatologist working there. He decided he liked the small desert town of about 25,000 people and decided to stay and open an office.

For many years he was the most prominent dermatologist in the area. He cared for patients from the local community, Nellis Air Force Base, the Nevada Test Site, and from a dozen distant frontier cow counties throughout Nevada from which patients had to travel hundreds of miles to see a doctor. He was prominent in many of the civic organizations in the city. I was not fully aware at the time of how much being in practice with him would benefit me in both my medical career and in the general community. I packed everything I owned into my brightly decorated hippy van, which still ran well, and tied a mattress on top of it, and drove from Madison to Las Vegas. I probably resembled a modern-day hippie version of Tom Joad. I had a thousand dollars in my pocket, and a good job waiting for me and was very happy.

Las Vegas is in the center of a desert valley that is about twenty miles wide and thirty miles long. The Spring Mountains are to the West. On the east side are the Frenchman Mountains and Sunrise Mountain. In the center of the valley is Las Vegas and the adjoining cities of North Las Vegas, Henderson, and Boulder City. There were about 300,000 people living in this metropolitan area. The Strip runs through the center of Las Vegas. It is several miles of casinos and hotels and party joints with lights that advertise that they never close and the fun never stops. When you drive into Vegas at night, the sky is glowing from miles away.

When you pass over the dark, barren mountain peaks the whole central valley jumps into view as a bright oasis in a ring of black hills. It is still miles to the valley floor, but you feel you are already there. I found a small apartment not far from the office in which I would be working. After the first several weeks, Dr. Boyer gave me an advance on my income so I could get some furniture and not have to sleep on my mattress on the apartment floor.

Our original office was on the east side of town on the corner of Charleston Blvd and Eastern Blvd and near the downtown area. It had been converted from an old apartment building and was too small a place for all three of us to work. We opened a second office on the west side of town close to the University Hospital. Dr. Boyer had a new sign built outside the office with all our names on it. It was the first practice of my own, and I was very happy having it displayed where everyone could see it.

The first year of living in Las Vegas went well. I got to know the other physicians in town, and they started sending some of their surgery cases to me. I joined the faculty of the University of Nevada School of Medicine, which had a division in Las Vegas, and started teaching medical students and residents and lecturing at meetings and at some of the local hospitals. As predicted, I became a member of the Rotary club. I even joined a local church. These were the days of mom and pop medicine. Almost all medical practices in town were one or two doctors working independently, often with family members helping out in the office. We worked under the name Dermatology Medical Associates.

Medical records were short handwritten notes on eight by five cards and filled in a cabinet and expanded as necessary. The initial office visit was fifteen dollars, and a follow-up visit was five dollars. Injections and any surgery required were additional. With three physicians, we were the largest dermatology group in town. One other practice had two physicians, Dr. Paulson and Dr. Landow. There were a few other solo dermatologists in the area.

One weekend a month, I would fly to Columbia, South Carolina, and spend it with my son, Hayes. After our separation, Beckay had quickly filed for divorce, and I did not protest it. We continued to have a cordial relationship, and both of us were glad the marriage was over. We last met twenty-five years ago at our son's high school graduation, but I still send her an alimony check each year since she never remarried. I asked my divorce attorney when the alimony would stop. She said when one of you dies. You are a successful doctor, and she is an underpaid school teacher, so just be happy it is not more. So each January, I still send her a check with the admonition to "live long and prosper."

After I had been working for a while, I calculated that I would make about $60,000 during my first year in practice. That was an impressive number to me. As a young boy in Ahoskie, my parents drove by the home of our physician one day. It was one of the largest in town. My father told me the doctor made over fifty thousand dollars a year. At that age I had no real concept about income levels or earning potentials, but he made it sound like a lot of money, and I was now in that category.

After a few years in Las Vegas, I married again. Her name was Missie. I had come to like southern Nevada much more than I anticipated and decided I might stay longer than the few years I had originally planned. Missie and I bought a ranch style house on a dirt road on an acre of desert outside of town, five miles from the nearest convenience store. It was remote with only a few nearby houses but with a variety of rattlesnakes, scorpions, tarantulas, and coyotes as occasional visitors. Those are things to which you eventually become accustomed. I had chickens and a fish pond and some fruit trees on the property. At night away from the city, the sky and land were wide open, and when the winds blew up, you could hear and feel the force of the Mohave desert sand moving around you.

Our front yard was miles of open range extending to the Spring Mountains, and when the storms moved through, it was a light and thunder show followed by flash floods through the several washes near our property. I bought tools and cowboy boots and a cowboy hat and worked my farm like a pioneer. I plowed up a garden to grow my own food. We considered having horses but decided that might be going a bit too cowboy.

After a few years, I got a call from Dr. Mohs. He was retiring and wanted to know if I would consider taking his place as the head of the Mohs Surgery department at the University of Wisconsin. That was a position I would have to consider since it was the motherland of his specialty. I took a flight from Las Vegas on a beautiful late fall day and landed in Madison in a blizzard. I toured the new surgical facility and hospital which had been built since I had been gone. It was an impressive place, and the offer was fair and it was an honor to be considered for the position, but I knew I was not coming here. On the flight back home it came to me that I was going to be in Las Vegas for the rest of my working career. If I turned down the best Mohs position in the world, it was because I loved my job where I was and the city and the people with whom I had become friends and partners. I was not a Las Vegas native. At this time almost everyone was from somewhere else, but I planned to stay long enough to make it my home.

In 1981 I was working in the clinic, and my receptionist came to my office and said there was someone on the telephone who wanted to talk to me.

"Who is that?" I asked.

"He says his name is Dr. George Grigsby, and he was wondering if you might know him," the receptionist replied.

Of course, I knew who he was but had not heard from him for about ten years since the time he moved north and I went west. I knew this was a good time to give my old friend a little teasing. I took the phone call. George said he had seen my name on the sign outside the office and wondered if I was from North Carolina and did I remember him.

I said, "George? George? I am not quite sure if I remember that name. Where do you come from again?"

## DR. GEORGE T. GRIGSBY AND DR. LUCIUS BLANCHARD

He told me he was from Holly Springs and said he was living in Las Vegas now. I said I kind of remember someone from there but was not sure. I suggested he come by the office the next day and we could go to lunch, and maybe I would remember better if I saw him in person. That was kind of fun.

George had finished his training in internal medicine at George Washington University and then moved to Boston for an additional year of training. He had been in the military service as chief of medicine at Forbes Air Force Base in Topeka, Kansas. As the sole surviving son of his branch of the Grigsby family line, he did not have to go to Vietnam. He had also worked in a local hospital emergency department in Topeka after he was discharged from the service. He had recently moved to Las Vegas to be a professional gambler, which was not working out as well as he had hoped. Gambling in person was harder than it looked on television. He also had to work in the emergency department of the University Medical Center, which was adjacent to one of our dermatology offices.

It was great seeing him again. I had little contact with many people from my undergraduate or medical school classes, so It was nice to have a friend back from those years, especially someone I liked and found interesting. Like me, he enjoyed skiing, and he had a house in Aspen, Colorado. He had acquired a large number of close friends during his years in Topeka and stayed in contact with them. He was a semi-KU fan since one of his best friends was the biggest donor to the KU athletic program, so he got to see the games from their private box with the coaches and university officials.

Neither of us had been back to Chapel Hill for several years, but we were both still active in supporting the medical school and were members of the alumni association and were annual donors to the medical school loyalty fund to support students with scholarships. George was better remembered than I was since he was one of the Black Pioneers at UNC. He was more artistically oriented than I was, and he also had an interest in supporting the Ackland Art Museum at UNC. I was more interested in supporting a winning basketball team, so we both had maintained connections with our alma mater. I was not surprised that George had never married. He had been with some very beautiful women, one named Tina I remembered from Rocky Mount, N.C., but he was never quite ready to take the final step in any relationship. He seemed to prefer his own way of living and independence. He was not able to make that fit in a permanent arrangement with another person.

He came from an extended family with many relatives, but he had no brothers or sisters. Now it seemed unlikely he would marry or have children. He would be the last of the Grigsby line on his dynastic branch. Even when George and I would travel together, he needed some individual time alone each day. We would manage our schedules to do some things together and then have some space to follow our own pursuits.

On one of our trips we decided to go to Amsterdam in the days when it was still a refuge for drop-outs and lost expats. When I was looking for hotel rooms in the city, I was surprised how hard they were to find and how expensive they were. I was able to find a small room in a nice hotel in the center of town for a truly exorbitant price but reserved it anyway. When we got to Amsterdam, we discovered we were there the week of the finals in a European soccer tournament.

The entire city was in soccer madness. Enthusiastic fans were everywhere, and every restaurant and shop had the matches on television. We were not soccer fans, but I decided we should go see one of the contests while we there.

I asked the hotel concierge if we could get any tickets. She said she could find us two tickets for about 1500.00 dollars each. That did not work out. We visited some of the brown cafes and the bars that sold marijuana and tried some of their wares instead and watched the game on television. It was a better use of our money. We saw the Red-Light District, which was sad. The museums were spectacular, especially for a van Gogh fan.

We rode bikes through the rain across a countryside covered with tulip fields, visited windmills, dikes, shallow seas, and had lunch in a village pub. It could not get any more Dutch. We had another interesting trip to Rio de Janeiro. We wanted to spend time on the exotic Brazilian beaches of Copacabana and Ipanema with the rich and beautiful and famous people in the world. Sadly, it rained almost every day we were there, and everyone was wearing rain gear and carrying umbrellas; not all that beautiful. We visited around the city to see the tourist sites and spent the afternoons in the bars drinking caipirinha cocktails. The poverty and the people begging in the streets was oppressive. The beautiful people were nowhere to be seen.

The most excitement we had was late one-night walking along Copacabana beach, returning to our hotel from a bar we had visited. Right outside our hotel we were jumped by a gang of young thieves. It was a sudden and unexpected attack. In just a few seconds, they stole George's Swatch watch off his arm and twenty dollars that I had in my pocket. I grabbed two of them and pulled them out into the street and was holding onto them.

A car stopped next to us, and a man jumped out with his pistol, and the youths fled immediately. I do not know if he was undercover police or just an armed citizen that stopped to help us, but he was there at the right time. The assault was irritating but not really harmful to either of us. Whenever I travel, I keep small amounts of money in many places, so my financial loss was minimal. The next day I saw one of the guys who robbed us sitting on a bench on the beach. He asked how I was doing and where my friend was. He did not offer to give me our stuff back, however. George decided we should go to Cuba. In the 1990s, that was off-limits to Americans; it was illegal to go there. So we went to Canada and took a flight from there to Havana. There was no problem getting through immigration, and they did not put stamps in our passports.

We were treated well everywhere we went. We spent a few days at a resort on the coast with excellent food and drinks and beautiful long beaches. In the small village of Varadero, there was Latin music and dancing at local theater groups and in the parks. People from many other places were vacationing there, especially from Canada and Europe. George and I were kind of unique. When we told people we were from Las Vegas, they looked surprised and said, "You're not supposed to be here, are you?"

We spent a day in Havana and saw the old city and the old cars from the 1950s. We met the old people who were suffering from the embargo put in place by the Americans after the failed Bay Of Pigs invasion. There were statues and photographs of Fidel and Che throughout the city. In the afternoon, we went to the El Floridita Bar in Old Habana.

It was the hangout for Ernest Hemingway, one of my favorite authors, and reputed to be the "cradle of the daiquiri."

I bought a round of drinks for everyone in the bar so we could drink a toast to "papa" Hemingway. That night we went to an elaborate floor and dinner show at the Copacabana club. It was a show right out of the Las Vegas gala reviews from the 1970s. George and I felt at home in Havana.

I took George on a fishing trip with some of my friends. He and I were not avid fishermen like they were, but we thought we would have a good time since we were going tarpon fishing off the Caribbean coast in Costa Rica. We took a small plane into a remote site at the mouth of the Coronado River and were put up in rustic camp buildings in the jungle. Each morning we went out in small boats to the fishing grounds in the ocean off the mouth of the river. I think I caught one tarpon, and I do not think George got any. However, it was an exciting trip. The first day one of my friends fell out of his boat into the rough ocean waves in the inlet. He had to be rescued, and fortunately, he was wearing a life jacket, or he would have been swept under the water quickly.

In the afternoon, storms came up with heavy tropical rains. I had a wet suit packed in my gear, so I was fine. Our guide made a temporary suit for George from a giant black garbage bag with holes cut out for his head and arms. George kept right on fishing. That night back at the camp, one of our group decided he had enough of the jungle and called for a private plane to pick him up. He was gone in a few hours. George and I were also tired of fishing in a few days. We decided to visit Tortuguero Park a few miles south of our camp. We arranged for a canoe to take us through the canals and mangrove swamps to the park site, a trip that took about a half-day. At the park, we had a nice cabin and a proper dining room.

The main reason we were here was to see the turtles. We were very fortunate that on the night we arrived there was a lot of activity. We hiked from the camp to the beach and waited until about midnight. Then the giant turtles came washing up through the ocean waves like slow-moving boulders. They crawled up the beach to an area that was above the high tide mark and began digging wide depressions in the sand with their flippers. When the hole was ready, they laid their eggs.

When the actual process of depositing the eggs happens, the turtles go into a trance and become unaware of what is around them. We were able to move up close to watch and actually touch them without any harm. After the eggs are laid, she covers them over with sand, and the mother retreats to the sea. Her job is finished, and she will not return to this beach until it is time to lay her eggs again.

We waited on the beach longer, and soon one of the nests of eggs that had been laid earlier in the season opened up, and dozens of baby turtles emerged and started their rush for the protection of the ocean. If they hatch during the day, few of the hatchlings will make it to the sea since many predators are waiting for them.

The ones that get there will still have a hazardous journey, and only a few will make it to adulthood. The ones that do will come back to this same beach to lay their eggs. George and I stayed at the camp for a day and looked for birds and golden poison frogs and really big jungle spiders. Then we got the small airplane that had daily flights back to San Jose and met up with our friends for the trip back to Las Vegas. Over the past 30 years, George and I had many other trips, including skiing in Aspen and Whistler and Park City.

He is a much better skier than am I. He has great form and grace and control. He is like an African-American Stein Ericksen, graceful with his knees and skis together all the time and controlled in his turns. I am usually faster but with less form and control and frequently get piled in a mound of snow.

We had a summer vacation trip to St. Barts, a very upscale French Caribbean island famous for stunning beaches, high-end shopping, restaurants, and luxury yachts. We went to one of their clothes optional beaches. It is very true that the sun and time and gravity had not been kind to most people there. We left and went to one of the seaside restaurants in Gustavia for happy hour and tropical cocktails. It was much more enjoyable scenery.

We went hiking in the Grand Canyon on the south rim. This canyon has been carved out of the sandstone rock of the Colorado Plateau by the Colorado River for the past six million years and is more than a mile deep. George and I hiked down the Bright Angel trail. There were few other people there, but at one point, we were confronted by a bighorn sheep with a full curl horn who thought he had possession of the path. It was a reminder of Billy Goat Gruff, so we retreated until he allowed us to pass. We climbed and bouldered at Red Rock Canyon and Mount Charleston just a few miles outside of Las Vegas. We spent time riding bikes and drinking on the sand at Newport Beach. We visited Panama and decided to become property owners there.

This was a very stable and calm period in my time in Las Vegas. Things were going well with my work and family and friends. I was President of the Nevada Chapter of the American Cancer Society and the Rotary Club and active in many other organizations. It was now time to start expanding our dermatology company in the rapidly growing city of Las Vegas.

# Chapter 14

That original year or two that I had planned to stay in Las Vegas was over forty years ago, and I still practice dermatology here full time. I was very fortunate to have a great deal of compatibility with both my original medical partners. The only disagreements we experienced were generational and based on our concepts for the future of the practice. My two partners were in their late sixties and appropriately were not planning for long term arrangements for our company. After I decided I was staying in Las Vegas, it became my responsibility to prepare our practice for the fundamental changes that were coming in the business world of medicine in the United States.

We made a formal agreement that we were all equal partners in the company. Financial provisions were included that would provide payments to the original partners when they left the practice. I would manage the company with their consent and advice for the coming future. We were able to navigate this successfully with almost no disruption. Break up of medical partnerships are frequently more bitter and expensive than family divorces. I had seen it multiple times when former medical partners who were close friends try to destroy each other after their separation. In both situations, the lawyers and accountants and competitors usually come out the winners. We all wanted to avoid that ending. I changed the name of our group to Las Vegas Skin and Cancer Clinics. This was to encompass the changing nature of dermatology to reflect the increasing performance of surgical procedures such as Mohs cancer surgery and cosmetic services.

The original name of our specialty was "Dermatology and Syphilology," from the importance in the past of the medical treatment of this disease as well as leprosy and psoriasis and other skin conditions. Many treatments for these conditions were recorded dating back to the time of ancient Egypt and Greece. As the prevalence of these conditions decreased, the training in dermatology changed also, and cutaneous surgery became an important part of the services provided by many dermatologists.

The other major addition to our practice was computers. These were in the early stages of development for medicine, but it was obvious they would be necessary to stay current with the coming changes. I did not like computers, and my knowledge of the world of medical computer systems was that there were hardware and software, and they were different. Our initial system was rudimentary and little more than an electronic database and billing system. It worked well enough and was an early training platform for the current system we now use that coordinates every aspect of the delivery of health care at all levels. When the computer is down, and we have to find a pen and piece of paper to record anything, even I miss using computers, but I still do not like them.

Dr. Boyer was right about the future of Las Vegas. Over the past forty years the city has been one of the fasting growing communities in the country. The mild climate and low tax burden and low cost of living drew people from all over the United States. People from California especially found it attractive as the cost of everything in that state exploded. At the height of growth, there were three thousand people a month moving to Clark County. There was a waiting list to get any utility services, and new homes were being auctioned to the highest bidder, and there was a waiting list for that. The population soon exceeded two million people.

In this environment, everyone had the opportunity to be successful, especially in the medical community. Even bad doctors were doing well since each month, there were three thousand new residents who did not yet know many of the physicians here were not very competent. At Las Vegas Skin and Cancer Clinics, there were changes over those years. As the city grew, we also expanded and eventually had seven locations in the valley.

Dr. Mori had a heart attack and sudden death early one morning. When his son called to tell me, I was only partially awake, and I thought for a brief time, we were talking about a patient who had died. Suddenly it came to me what had happened. It was an unexpected loss of a friend and business partner and fellow dermatologist. He did not have a history of heart disease; unfortunately, sometimes, the first symptom is sudden death.

Dr. Boyer retired after many years of practice. He was one of the most prominent people in town, not only as a physician but as a businessman and community leader. He was active in many civic organizations. Several years after retirement, he was diagnosed with intestinal cancer and died shortly afterward. I was privileged to be one of the speakers at his memorial service. He had been a great partner and mentor to me for many years. As our practice expanded, additional physicians joined our company. I was also aware of the new trend in having physician assistants in medical practices, but some of our older established doctors were sure this was not proper. How could a PA with two years of general medical training compare to an MD who had intensive education for a minimum of seven years in medicine and dermatology? I was in favor of adding a PA to our practice. I had the advantage of having worked with medics like Bop in the Army and with ex-military PAs in emergency rooms and was comfortable that they could adequately provide good medical care.

Many of these early physician assistants came from a military background. We began with one new PA who had worked in a dermatology office in California. He taught us how to use a mid-level provider. It took Dr. Boyer a year to even acknowledge his presence, but eventually, he had to agree the guy did pretty well. Now Las Vegas Skin and Cancer has mid-level providers in all our offices with excellent success.

The other major event we faced in Las Vegas was the change in the point of access to medical care from being direct with a personal doctor to access being controlled by the insurers and HMOs. Patients previously were able to choose their physician and see them as they desired and receive treatment as determined by the patient and physician. Insurance companies and Medicare would then pay the doctor directly.

With their effort to reduce medical expenses and to increase the control and profits of the insurance companies and the medical management companies, patients became "members" of a medical organization that controlled which doctors the patient could see, what treatment would be appropriate for their medical condition and how much the doctor would be paid for his services. This was happening nationally as well as in Las Vegas.

Physicians were no longer in direct control of their patient's care since the management companies had to approve treatments. Patients could no longer see a physician of their choice unless that physician was approved and had a contract as a "medical provider" with that particular management company. This was a source of intense disagreement in the medical community in Las Vegas. Some physicians refused to become associated with any of the HMOs and would not refer patients to any physician that did. Some physicians were afraid not to join with the HMOs since they might lose access to their current patients who were being forced into the HMO for their medical care. For some doctors, the loss of income, since the HMOs paid a reduced amount of money for medical care, could severely damage their profitability. For some physicians, it seemed this was the future of medicine, and the days of the small independent mom and pop medical provider were fading away and not sustainable.

This became divisive in our group. Fortunately, dermatology was not initially affected as much as primary care providers, and we thought we had some time to see what the outcome would be. Our older doctors said they would never practice under rules that told them who they could see and what they could do; they thought no one would agree to that, not doctors or patients. I thought this change would occur no matter how much we protested, and it was better to get ahead of the curve if possible.

Since we were the largest and most respected dermatology group in Las Vegas, the HMOs wanted to have us in their system and offered us reasonable terms if we would agree to be part of their provider network. After frequent discussions in our group, we decided that was the prudent path for us to take. There was criticism from some doctors in the community who were against this, and some of them stopped referring their patients to our practice. In the long run, however, it was a decision that let us grow even larger and plan for expansion that would be very beneficial to Las Vegas Skin and Cancer in the future.

Missie and I lived on our little desert ranch for a dozen years. We had a daughter we named Sarah after Missie's younger sister, who had died early from aggressive breast cancer. Later we were divorced. Work was requiring my time, and she became involved in philanthropic organizations helping to rehabilitate disabled and recovering alcoholics. Our interests and ambitions slowly but irrevocably diverged until we decided it was better to follow separate paths but remain friends and good parents. That is still working well.

George stayed in Las Vegas, and we continued to be close friends. His career as a professional gambler was still not going well, so he joined the Veterans Administration as a physician. The income and benefits were very good. Doctors at the VA get a lot of vacation days and holidays off. Meanwhile, I was working harder than ever managing the expansion of our dermatology group and having to spend more time in administrative work as well as seeing patients. I could tell I would need to make some changes.

As George and I were getting into our fifth decade and both still had excellent health, we decided we should become more adventurous in the good years we had left. It was not exactly a bucket list like Jack Nicholson and Morgan Freeman devised, and I could not get George to join me on all of them. One of my medical partners and I decided we would like to be pilots, so we bought an airplane. I had about 10 hours of training before deciding to give it up.

I have been a certified scuba diver for years and thought George should try it. We went to Ambergris Key in Beliz for his training, but after an hour he and his instructor decided it was not going to be successful.

I thought we should become skydivers. I made three solo jumps, which were exciting but not something I would want to continue. George was not too interested, but for his birthday I gave him a gift certificated for a tandem jump at the

Boulder City airport outside of Las Vegas. He finally made the leap. He landed alive and well with a giant smile on his face, either from relief that he was back on the ground or because it was a major thrill.

I wanted to climb one of the Seven Summits, so I went to Africa and reached the top of Mt. Kilimanjaro. I wanted to go where there had been only few travelers, and I arranged a camel safari for my family and me into the remote parts of Kenya where there were no permanent settlements, and the nomadic herders did not need to wear clothes.

I went to Libya while it was still safe under the tight control of Gaddafi and traveled through the Sahara Desert with a native Tuareg tribe who were clothed in their purple dress and decorations. While there, I bought some long white flowing robes in a local store and a white turban and rode for several days on a camel through the tall pyramid-shaped sand dunes and pretended my name was Lawrence.

A few years ago, I was able to get permission to spend two weeks in North Korea and traveled under the strict control of Kim Jong-Un and bowed down to his stature or portrait whenever I was near one.

I went to Bhutan, the location of James Hilton's "Lost Horizon" utopian Shangri-La, and meditated with the Buddhist monks for several weeks. Sadly, I did not have the intense training the monks receive in their monasteries from the time they are small children, and my meditation time frequently became short naps.

I want on a mountain expedition trip to Tibet, and climbed up to the advanced base camp on Mt. Everest, at 21,000 feet. Nothing I can think of could have made me go any higher.

George and I did go to Dubai. We did not stay at the Burj Al Arab, which was about two thousand dollars a night, but we had dinner at the restaurant on top of it. I ordered a Bloody Mary, which costs thirty-five dollars, and told George we could not look at the prices on the dinner menu; just order something and let it be a surprise when we get the bill. That must have worked because neither of us remember what we ate or how much dinner cost us. You go there for the view, not the food or Bloody Marys. My family and I traveled on an icebreaker to Antarctica. Penguin colonies are more photographic and attractive and less smelly on television than in person. We went to China before many tourists were there and almost everyone had bicycles instead of cars. My seven-year-old daughter with blue eyes and long blond hair was a photographic sensation. Many Chinese families had their photograph taken with her and wanted to touch her silky straight hair. I got married for the third time. Her name is Amy, and she used to work in our medical office.

Entering my sixth decade, things were going better than I had expected. My children had greatly exceeded my minimal requirements for them, which was to reach majority without a criminal record or drug dependence. Both were college graduates. Hayes was in the Peace Corp in Armenia and would live and work in Europe and the Middle East for the next twenty-five years. Sarah went to medical school at the University of North Carolina, did her residency training at Duke University, and would become a Pediatric Dermatologist. Amy and I were still married.

I had some money saved in the bank and was financially secure. George was in a similar situation. He was working part-time at the VA hospital and was planning for full retirement in a few years. His farmland and business properties were in Holly Springs which had grown from a wide spot on a two-lane rural highway into a highly desirable upscale bedroom community for the Research Triangle. This was gentrification at its most profitable.

It was time for us to consider what our exit strategy would be like. I had to find a way to continue the success of Las Vegas Skin and Cancer without me. George and I were frequent visitors to the UNC campus for football games and basketball games and class reunions. Both of us were long time legacy donors to the medical school, and both of us wanted to become more involved with Carolina and leave a lasting contribution to the place that had been so influential in our success.

My efforts to have a successful exit strategy would be more stressful and time-consuming than I had ever anticipated. The things you remember in old age are not the time you bought a stock, and it doubled in value or the piece of vacant land you owned that became a housing development. It is the things that wake you at four in the morning, wondering how you can possibly make it work. My answer to that would be baby steps.

# Chapter 15

It was the debt; the kind of debt that destroys ambitions and steals peaceful sleep. Most people have experienced it at some level. In this case, it ran into millions of dollars to multiple creditors. I had always managed Las Vegas Skin and Cancer in a conservative fiscal manner. I avoided borrowing money and was willing to delay or forego any obligations that we could not pay immediately out of the current company cash flow.

This created a very strong balance sheet and credit rating for us since we had no outstanding loans. This is not always the smartest way to operate. The prudent use of debt can be very beneficial to a company planning on expansion and with the resources to do it safely. That is what one of my dermatology colleagues was trying to do in California.

Las Vegas Skin and Cancer was a strong company but had the problem that it depended entirely on one individual to keep it operating, and I was reaching my mid-sixties. There was no obvious exit strategy in sight.

One problem with transitioning a medical practice with multiple providers and offices is that a patient's relationship is usually with an individual doctor and not the company for which that doctor works. So the highest value of the company is in keeping all the medical providers and their patients in the organization. Most doctors are highly competitive people. They have been so since grade school. If not, they would not have become as successful as are most of them. They can also be difficult to manage. The saying in the medical profession is that trying to manage doctors is like trying to herd cats. They always have the propensity to run off.

In the time of mom and pop medical offices, the incoming new young doctors would buy out the old retiring ones. That is what I did with my senior partners. That scenario was not workable for Las Vegas Skin and Cancer. I offered to sell the company, in part or in its entirety, to any of our doctors, but none of them were interested. There was no reason they should buy it. All of them were doing very well financially, and they did not need the problems and stress of running the business or the risk and expense of buying it. At any time they could leave and open an independent office next door and do just as well. In Nevada non-compete restriction clauses in a doctor's employment contracts are almost never enforceable; only attorneys benefit from trying to uphold them. When an offer to buy the company came from an outside source, I was very surprised and happy. This was in the early days of consolidation of small dermatology offices into big groups by entrepreneurial investors. Dr. Robert West, a dermatologist in Southern California, had built up an organization of about twenty-five dermatology offices in California, Arizona, and a few other states in the mid-West. He wanted to expand into Nevada, and he would buy my company. He asked how much I wanted for Las Vegas Skin and Cancer and how I would structure the sale.

This was a new area in which I had to operate. I did some quick self-taught education in how to value and sell a medical company, got some advice from our accountant and company lawyer, and from some local business leaders in the medical community. Most of them did not have much experience in this area since it was a new business concept. Of course, despite my educational efforts, I was still a neophyte in this arena. I constructed what seemed to be a reasonable value for Las Vegas Skin and Cancer and then gave them an asking price of twice as much. They accepted it. In the series of meetings, we had over the next few months, I met Dr. West, who was an older gentleman, devoutly Mormon, and completely honest. He had three sons who were also dermatologists. One of them worked with him in California. It also became apparent that the acquisition process was being driven by his financial advisor and manager of West Dermatology and that Dr. West was more of a figurehead. I had only a few dealings with him directly. I worked closely with one of his associates, Anthony, who was given the responsibility of closing the acquisition.

This process went smoothly, and since Las Vegas Skin and Cancer was a debt-free and profitable company, it was an easy analysis for them. I agreed to a substantial down payment and that I would carry a promissory note for the remainder of the purchase price. This would turn out to be a big miscalculation on my part. I discussed this with all my associate physicians, and none of them objected to the transition since it did not affect their income. It appeared to give Las Vegas Skin and Cancer the long-term stability it needed to continue after I was gone. I signed the papers, and we became Las Vegas Skin and Cancer Clinics, a division of West

Dermatology. I cashed my check for the initial down payment and started considering how I would use the extra free time and income I would have since West Dermatology would now manage the business. That would turn out to be an unnecessary calculation.

Initially, the financial agreement went well. After the first year, however, West Dermatology began having difficulty making the payments due on their promissory note to me. Frequently it would be delayed or only be a partial payment. Anthony became more seriously involved in running Las Vegas Skin and Cancer, and internally things continued smoothly. The clinic was always able to provide quality medical care to the patients. Occasionally management would get behind in paying some office expenses but not serious enough to disrupt the clinical operation.

I infrequently met Dr. West to discuss the payment shortfalls, but it was becoming apparent that he was getting even less aware of the status of the company being operated under his name. Almost everything was being orchestrated by his administrative staff and, to some extent, by his wife. I was concerned about the ability of West Dermatology to manage the current cash requirements but was still getting payments regularly enough that I did not think I had any reason to become more involved immediately. The long-term goal of companies like West was to accumulate a large enough book of business to attract a buyer such as a private equity group that would purchase it, hopefully for a large profit. West was an attractive target since it had multiple offices in half a dozen states. It had an impressive annual revenue. It owned a pathology laboratory and a billing company.

With all these advantages, a medium-size private equity investor decided to examine West as a possible acquisition target. I was very glad to see that since it seemed to confirm the value of the company. If they acquired West, they would also pay off the remainder of the note owed to me. I had multiple conversations with the investors since the Las Vegas part of the company was now the largest revenue producer in the West Company and was showing the fastest growth. We were an important part of the equation to ensure the continued success of the company.

As the private equity group performed their extensive analysis of West Dermatology, several things came into focus. Questions came up about the appropriateness of some of the accounting procedures and the possibility that some money had been diverted to unapproved uses and persons in the company. There was also concern that some medical billing had been submitted to insurance carriers and government agencies which, if audited, could result in substantial revenue take-backs and possible criminal investigation and large fines.

The debt the company was carrying to multiple lenders totaled millions of dollars and was a constant drain on West Dermatology and its operating capital. The private equity group, after spending a million dollars in analysis expenses, decided there was too much risk for them to proceed and withdrew their purchase offer.

I had a conversation with the head analyst from the equity group after they had made their decision to withdraw. He said he had a lot of respect for the Las Vegas portion of West but had many concerns about the viability of the company as an entity. Most of the growth of West Dermatology had been built on huge loans and speculation, the infamous house of cards. Specifically, he said they had never spent this much time and money for due diligence on a target acquisition and then decided to withdraw. Such a conversation did not reassure me about the security of my personal arrangement with the company.

This information caused a rapidly escalating crisis in West Dermatology over the next few months. Some of the top-level managers were removed or quit. Anthony stayed with the company out of loyalty to Dr. West and me. The banks that had made extensive loans were in the position of having to declare them "at-risk loans," putting the company and Dr. West personally in danger of bankruptcy. If this happened, the debt owed to me would also be eliminated, and West Dermatology would be taken into receivership by the court. Any remaining value I had in the company would be extinguished.

It was my negligence in accepting their purchase offer without doing a more extensive evaluation of the financial health of West Dermatology to see if they could afford to service the additional debt. Now it was my problem to deal with the consequences of my failure. Dr. West was becoming increasingly more impaired and not able to see patients or assist with the management of his company. His personal financial state was no longer able to support the continuing debts of West Dermatology. His three sons who were all dermatologists decided to leave West and open offices elsewhere.

Anthony and the accountants and the lawyers came to see me with a proposal I was expecting but was not expecting to like. They had devised a plan that I would become the new owner of West Dermatology so it could continue to operate. Anthony would stay on as the CEO and help with the management details. This is what I had been expecting, and it was difficult to find much that was favorable to me.

Now in my late sixties, I had successfully navigated the empire-building stage of my life and was not eager to start over again. The risks were massive with big debts to be resolved. The present income level of West was not even adequate to cover the operating expenses. There would be no additional capital available to help fund the recovery except for my income and savings accounts. The lenders might decide to call all the outstanding loans, triggering an immediate bankruptcy filing. If even one of our large revenue-producing medical offices decided to leave West, the company might be so cash-poor, it could not pay all the doctors, and then other physicians would also leave. There were a lot of cats out there. I could have the whole plan wrong. I might not be smart enough to do it. I might die before it could be completed. The main asset I could bring was the willingness to work hard and to believe it could be successful when others doubted. And I have always been lucky.

In chaos and crisis, there is opportunity. I had some income sources other than dermatology that I could rely on for ordinary living expenses. I had some money in savings that I could use to support the company in an immediate need. I had the support of Anthony and from my accountant Chris who was an excellent financial advisor and business resource for me. There were three hundred employees who worked at West, many who had years of experience and offered loyal support and would stay with the company.

Most importantly, I thought that Dr. West was correct in his vision, but poor in its execution. The opportunity for consolidation in the dermatology field was unlimited. Most practices were one or a few doctors working independently. They would all be potential acquisitions as the dermatology field became more consolidated. A few other entrepreneurs were doing the same thing in other parts of the country. Although it was insolvent, West Dermatology was the largest dermatology group in the south west. With great trepidation, I agreed to consider their plan but with much more diligence than I had used before. Fool me twice, shame on me.

I knew very few of the company doctors personally outside of those in Las Vegas. I had met several casually at some of the company holiday parties. These were the people I would have to convince to stay if there was any chance of continuing West Dermatology as a large operating group. I could not do it by myself.

I planned an impromptu road trip to visit the offices with the highest income and most respected doctors in the group. I planned it as a combination introduction, fact-finding, and begging pilgrimage. I needed to meet the physicians and let them know the plans Anthony and Dr. West were proposing but avoid discussing how fragile the financial situation really was. If they knew that, some of them might leave West or attempt to form a separate company of their own.

It would be an unobtrusive way of presenting myself. I wanted to make it a short, low profile appearance on my part; not a big deal, I was in the neighborhood and just stopping to say hello and let you know I would be helping out Dr. West in running the company. No big changes were in the works, just introducing myself. Please don't leave West Dermatology was the unstated message.

Only one doctor in San Diego refused to see me on my unscheduled visit to the front desk of his office. He said he was too busy to talk, but his waiting room was almost empty. I knew by reputation he had an arrogant personality, so I quietly left, giving his office manager a note for him explaining I was sorry he could not see me and apologized for the unscheduled visit. Within a short time, the doctor called me, asking if we could still get together. I think he had talked with some of the other West Dermatology doctors and suspected there was more going on than a drop-in.

I had been expecting this call, and I was still waiting in his parking lot but told him I was no longer available and would get back with him at a later time. It was an easy, risk-free way of making a power statement that the other doctors would hear about. All the other physicians that I talked with were either non-committal or not opposed to my becoming more involved in managing the company. The company accountant and financial advisor took me to visit the major banks who were lenders of millions of dollars to West Dermatology and Dr. West personally. There were some other debt holders that were individuals who were owed smaller amounts but who were not in a position to threaten West Dermatology's viability.

From the lenders' position, the loans were already in bankruptcy since the financial statement of West Dermatology did not show enough income to make the required loan payments. However, the bankers would do anything reasonable to avoid having to actually call in the loans for full payment. That would be removing the bottom support level on the house of cards.

They did not want to have to liquidate a medical company that would cost them expensive legal fees with little chance for recovery of any money for them. My accountant and lawyers convinced the banks to give me some time to see if the company could be restructured. Anthony and the financial advisors worked up a financial plan and spreadsheet that showed how the company could become profitable in about two years if it could continue in operation. I had a final meeting with my personal advisor, Chris, in his office, just the two of us. I asked him what I should do. When I ask Chris a question, I am going to get a long thought out answer. He calls it getting down in the weeds. I am going to learn a lot by just listening. I did not really expect him to tell me what to do. I decided I should try to save it. It was either possible failure for the company if I tried, or failure for sure if I did not.

I made the proposal to Anthony and Dr. West with the final outline of my requirements to close the proposed transaction. I would become President of the company. I would have one hundred percent ownership of everything in West Dermatology. That would not be just my previous Las Vegas offices but all the offices in California, Nevada, Arizona, Idaho, and a few other states, and the laboratory and billing company. I would pay Dr. West a small amount of money, mostly symbolic, to liquidate his ownership position. I would not assume any personal liability for any of the outstanding debts. Anthony and I alone would manage the company.

We arranged a formal meeting with the doctors I had previously visited and told them what would happen. I would support the company if they all stayed on. I would be only the temporary custodian, long enough to find a new buyer for West. They would all be given an opportunity to own stock in whatever new company that eventually bought us.

It was begging at its finest and was mostly successful. We only lost one provider who would not stay. She was a high maintenance diva who was not profitable for the company, so I didn't mind her leaving. The transaction was done. I was now in charge again and responsible for an even larger company.

All the projections and plans and preparations that I thought would promote success quickly fell apart. It would soon be the most stressful and expensive and prolonged business challenge I had ever faced. That is even considering that I used to try to make money owning and racing thoroughbred horses. Do you know how to have a small fortune in thoroughbred racing? Start with a large fortune. The debt was the destroyer of my plans and the thief of my peaceful sleep. The initial drain on my savings account was substantial. Each night I went to bed knowing that tomorrow I would have to make enough money to pay the rent and expenses of thirty offices and three hundred employees and the banks for another day. If I didn't make enough money, there would have to be another withdrawal from my personal account. If there was not enough ready cash available, then I had to decide which asset I could liquidate this time. For four years, I took no payments for my patient care. All of that money went back to support West Dermatology. After four years, most of the savings and other assets I had were almost exhausted.

I have never understood or trusted spreadsheets and the accuracy of their projections. One little adjustment on a small entry line, valid or not, over a long duration can change a loss into a profit in the last right-hand column of the page. Our two-year profitability plan was a spreadsheet illusion. The decision to bring in the expert and expensive employees and consultants to make an immediate and dramatic change for improved results became a money swamp. Occasional outside investors who evaluated West quickly lost interest. Those frequent early mornings when the anxiety attacks woke me at four o'clock when I would rather be still asleep, I adopted a new mantra. Baby steps-baby steps-baby steps; today, we will take a few baby steps; that's all. I hired a new CEO with the goal of eliminating redundant personnel and cutting expenses. I added several new sources of income that helped improve cash flow. Offices that were not significantly profitable were sold or closed. Slowly, very slowly, with baby steps, the company changed its direction.

At night, after work, I would take time to visualize a ship floating on the ocean. In my mind, she was the USS West. She was deep in the water but no longer slipping under as fast. Leaks were being sealed, unnecessary ballast was being discarded, and new fuel was being added. USS West was not yet a profitable vessel, but now I knew she would not become salvage.

It will seem odd that this mental image was more reassuring than all the accounting and balance sheets and profit and loss statements I was reviewing. Those were useful to the accountants, but to me, I could feel internally that the ship was stable again and would recover. I was glad that I had decided to be the temporary captain and help make it happen. The recovery of West continued slowly, and the trend that Dr. West was anticipating in dermatology was growing. He had died a few years earlier and would not get to see his plan eventually successful. A private equity group from New York contacted me. They were looking for medium size medical groups that could be expanded with an infusion of expert management and low-cost capital. They thought dermatology was the most promising specialty for this investment.

I sent them some basic financial statements and expected not to hear any more from them. Instead, they asked if I could meet with some of their principals. I was still not expecting any offers, but I agreed to meet them at a restaurant at the Las Vegas airport so they could have a quick turnaround, and I would not need to spend much time with them. After a little introduction and general discussion, they asked how much I thought West Dermatology was worth.

For obvious reasons, I had not given this any recent thought, so I used a number fifteen times higher than I thought it was really worth. They suggested that was a number they could work with for the possible purchase of the company. I was both surprised and skeptical. The purchase price I suggested was only a made-up number. From a strictly financial evaluation, West Dermatology had no real value. It did not make a profit and had no positive EBITDA; a number finance people use to value a company. I still had to put money in the organization to keep it open, and still took no income for my work. I never knew if the investors thought they were getting a bargain price or were overpaying. The negotiations were complicated and took about six months before the final papers were signed. This time I hired the most expert advisors I could find. Fool me twice, shame on me. I had heard stories about the private equity groups that buy a company and strip it of all its value for their profits. I had the impression this was not their plan, which made the deal easier for me.

Once again, I made an introducing and begging trip to all our major offices and received the support of all our doctors. When the deal was closed, I was able to recover all of the money I had put in the company and some profit. West Dermatology had all its debts paid off. The new owners held West for five years and were able to increase the number of offices by fifty percent and triple the amount of annual revenue the company earned. When we sold it again, they had quadrupled their investor's capital. I was also going to get a very good return on my shares of West Dermatology and some ownership in the new owner's investment fund. As promised, all of our doctors had been given the opportunity to buy stock in the new West Dermatology entity. The ones that did doubled their investment in two years and were given the opportunity to continue ownership in the new owner's investment fund if they wanted.

My night time anxiety attacks were a thing of the past. The USS West had been refurbished and sailed magnificently out of my imagination. The baby steps I had to take were replaced by big strides. It was a ten-year story in which I was an important player, but the real recovery work was done by all our staff and medical providers and the investors who took the risk and put in resources I never could. It worked out successfully for all of us, everyone. Once again, I was very lucky.

# Chapter 16

George had finished his career at the VA clinic and retired to the happy life of a real estate manager, an investor, and contemplator of the choices in life. His Pack House, the country store owned by his family in Holly Springs, had been closed for years. It was put on the list of historical places in North Carolina that should be preserved and renovated.

Several projects are under consideration since the town is now a thriving and expanding part of the Triangle area. Maybe it will become the Pack House brewing company or the Pack House Organic Restaurant or a place for a Grigsby art gallery and local history museum celebrating the accomplishments of the African American community after the Civil War.

It will seem difficult for the current generation to understand the importance of the country general store to a community and why it could be a historical landmark. Today everyone has an automobile, and there is a Walmart or convenient store within a short drive. The sight of someone, usually African American, walking along a country road, maybe with their children or elderly relatives, to visit the general store is largely a memory, something you might see in a Rockwell painting. At its time, it was the center of the community. The church and the general store were usually the first things to start a railroad crossing town in rural North Carolina. The Pack House was the source of food supplies, information and gossip, music and dancing, and sodas, and the fixings to run a still if there was one in the woods behind the farmhouse; and there were lots of them.

I had finished the final stage in the sale of West Dermatology and was only a small stock owner, not enough to have to stay on the directors' board or even go to meetings. I continued to work as a physician and medical director. I had twice made the transition from practicing medicine to managing medicine and back again. I liked dermatology and Mohs Surgery better than long business meetings and was happy and relieved to know I would spend my remaining working years doing what I enjoyed. The company was very successful, and I could work as much or as little as I wanted. George and I continued to spend time doing things we enjoyed. He was not a big sports fan, so I had to keep him up to date on how the Tar Heels were doing. Sometimes I would ask him if he watched the game on television. He never did because he is the only person I know who has never had a television set in his home. The university usually got us tickets to a football game each year with seats in the Chancellor's guest box. That is an exciting trip each year. Sometimes we got to sit courtside at basketball games in the Dean Dome. Dean Smith, George's old friend, was a long-time coach for UNC and one of the greatest of all time. He would be on the Mount Rushmore of college basketball coaches if there was one.

George and I made frequent trips to Panama. We both liked the country and the people there. He and I, along with a few other friends, bought a condominium in a high-rise building overlooking the city and Panama Bay. From our panoramic windows on the thirty-third floor, we can watch the sunrise over the Pacific Ocean. Do you know the only place in North and South America where there is no continental divide? In the middle of the Panama Canal, raindrops can flow to either ocean. Panama is a funny little country. I bought a small retirement home in the historical section of Panama City and an old hotel and restaurant that needed renovation. This would be my retirement job. I have always wanted to be a bar supervisor. The long and focused goal of becoming a doctor usually means people in the medical profession tend to become a specialist with few other passions. I wanted to be a doctor who could successfully remove a melanoma from a patient and also make a great Bloody Mary for a retired Panama pensionado.

George and I frequently visit UNC and Chapel Hill. His home in Holly Springs is a short drive away, and I have a house near campus where my daughter lived while she was at Carolina in medical school. Both of us were eager to continue supporting our university and medical students. As a result of the sale of West Dermatology, I had some discretionary capital to donate to UNC, so we began a scholarship program to recruit the best students in the country to come to Carolina.

The medical school at UNC is ranked as the number one primary care training hospital in the United States by the US News rankings. Each year it receives many more applications for admission than it can accept. A few of these are so outstanding that they will be accepted at any school to which they apply. They are the first-round draft picks in medical school student selection. They were the ones we wanted to recruit with a generous scholarship offer. George and I would never have made this lottery. In our days at the medical school, he was a middle-round selection, and I was a walk-on. So, this was our opportunity to hang out with the superstars and help our school too. Over the years, there have been about forty students to accept the medical school scholarship offer. Each of them have their full tuition paid, a ten-year interest-free loan to cover some of their living expenses, and an enrichment grant to pursue an independent goal of their own choosing.

Successful applicants have come from all over the world. They are all academic scholars, but that is only the beginning. These are students who have already made a difference. One man was a Dreamer from Mexico who was undocumented. Another came from an orphanage in Africa. Some have helped with refugees from Central America, with sex workers from Asia and with underserved African Americans in the United States. Some had been teachers and religious leaders and professional athletes. This is talent at its finest. In return, they are asked to always support Carolina with their loyalty and their presence and their gifts. That is always an easy sell.

## DR. GEORGE T. GRIGSBY AND DR. LUCIUS BLANCHARD

Each year, George and I, Bill from the University Foundation, the Dean of the Medical School, the Chancellor of UNC, and some members of the UNC medical faculty have an informal celebration dinner in Chapel Hill. All the newest scholarship students come as well as many of the present and past recipients to have a family get together. We are a small family group that is part of the greater Carolina Family. It is one of the happiest gatherings of the year for all of us.

George and I were visiting the campus for a class reunion in the spring of 2018. One of the events was held in the Carolina Inn, a hotel on the university campus. This is an elegant Colonial-style building that is listed on the National Register of Historic Places. It was built by a Carolina alumnus, John Sprunt Hill, in 1924 and donated to the University in 1935. Many school functions, weddings and parties, and club banquets are held there. It has the tradition of being the university's living room.

George and I frequently attend meetings in the Carolina Inn banquet rooms. About half the time, he remarks that when he ate here as a medical student, he would sometimes be mistaken for one of the colored wait staff and asked to carry a dinner tray for a white customer. He would politely correct them and find someone who could assist them. Then I usually reply that now he is being invited to come because he is an important and honored Black Pioneer at UNC, so I guess in the long run, things kind of even out. George and I are both in our late seventies, so we recycle some of our conversations. It is okay; both of us enjoy it.

After our lunch banquet, we walked down Columbia Street to Franklin Street and the downtown area. On the way, we went to the Ackland Art Museum. One of George's friends had a temporary exhibition in the museum showing works from his collection, so we stopped for a short visit to see his paintings. George likes the fine arts, especially the moderns.

About half the time we are in the Ackland, I remark that he should fund a Grigsby wing at the museum as his lasting memorial to the university. He expects this; he has heard it multiple times before, but it still brings a smile to his face. But no Grigsby gallery yet. The trust for the museum was originally donated by William Hayes Ackland. He was from Tennessee and wanted the people of his native south to know and love the fine arts. He wanted to always stay close to and remain a part of his endowment. He originally willed it to

Duke University, but their trustees declined it because they did not like some of the terms of the bequest. Eventually, it was established on the campus at UNC. The museum opened in 1958 and was extensively renovated in 1990, making it one of the most prominent university art museums in the south. Recently it received a twenty-five million donations of artworks and trust funds to continue its important function. In accordance with William Ackland's final wishes, he has remained close to his museum. He is buried in Gallery 3, just to the left of the main lobby.

Franklin Street borders the north side of McCorkle Place, an open quad known as the university's front yard and home to many historical monuments. The most famous of these is the Old Well, located across from South Building. It is where the original students got their drinking water, and it is the iconic symbol of UNC. Drinking from the fountain will ensure your wisdom and academic success. There are sometimes lines of students there at the beginning of each semester, hoping it will work. At the other end of McCorkle's place is the statue of Silent Sam. In the eight years George and I lived in Chapel Hill we have walked by Sam hundreds of times with little notice of him standing there quietly keeping watch from the top of his pedestal. This time we saw he was surrounded by dozens of people, including several police officers. He was plastered with home-made posters and placards and covered in some areas with red paint. I said," George, we have to go over there. Maybe they are having some kind of demonstration". It reminded me of the anarchy from the 1960s, with civil disobedience and the destruction of public property but now with everyone taking "selfies."

Actually, I was proud of the participants. For years I had said that the recent generations of students were more interested in board rooms and six-figure incomes than in making a difference in the world. My admiration was partly nostalgic and partly realism. I would have liked to join them, but also, I knew that I had become part of the establishment against whom they were demonstrating.

Silent Sam came to Carolina in 1913 as a gift from the Daughters of the Confederacy. He is a young bronze Confederate shoulder who stands at the front of McCorkle's place and the entrance to the university campus. He faces to the north, watching for a ghostly return of the bluecoat Union Army to invade the south. His ammunition pouch is empty so he cannot fire the rifle he is holding; hence he is

Silent. He was placed there to remember the thousands of UNC students and faculty who left the school to join the Confederate Army and to honor all those who were never able to return.

Who is Silent Sam? He is a young southerner at the University of North Carolina who became a soldier and joined the Confederate Army out of pride for his native home and to protect it from the Union invaders who wanted to conquer and occupy his homeland. As a youth before the Civil war, he worked on his family farm or small-town business. He could not afford to own slaves or much land or have a large income.

He could not afford to buy his way out of military service, and his patriotism would not have let him do so even if he could have. If he survived the carnage of the war, possibly with injuries or illness, he returned home to recover and rebuild his life and family as well as possible. For most Confederates returning from the Civil War there were no welcoming ceremonies or parades or celebrations for the soldiers who had lost the war. He deserves the respect due soldiers who have risked all and sometimes given all in service to their country and what they believed to be necessary. To remove Silent Sam would be trying to eradicate an important part of our history and culture.

Who is Silent Sam? He is an unrepentant symbol of generations of white masters that unlawfully and immorally enslaved four million people of color. He fought in the Civil war, and despite abolition and the surrender of his Confederate Army, he supported the continued subrogation of former slaves through intimidation and repression. He advocated white supremacy as a matter of birthright and the will of the Lord.

He and other Confederate southerners have been inappropriately honored by statures and named locations. Polk place, the main quad on campus, was named after James K. Polk, a UNC graduate in 1818, the eleventh President of the United States and a slave owner and a strong promoter of its continuation. The presence of Sam on the campus of a university that is supposed to represent equality and to be a place "for all people" is an affront to all people of any ethnic origin and should be removed by any possible means including civil disobedience.

I told George we had to get a photograph of ourselves in this new protest movement. We got one of the participants to take it for us. We reversed roles. I kneeled at the base of the monument in the current fashion of "taking the knee," and George stood over me, like the "man" keeping me down. It was "bottom rail on top, this time." Sadly, the era of Reconstruction died quickly through a resurgence of white supremacy, and any advances in equality were replaced by Jim Crow regulations and KKK intimidation.

George and I had our photograph. It is a picture of an old black man and an old white man fondly remembering and reliving their days. To these students surrounding Sam, we would be kind of interesting, and they would be slightly amused at our reconstruction. They could not see us sixty years ago, demonstrating in this same place for some of the same idealist goals. That photograph taken here sixty years ago would have been of us marching with protest signs, wearing long hair and beards and railing against the police and National Guard. If we could have shown these protesting students that old photograph, I wonder what they would think of this black man and white man standing by the stature today.

That was our time. I wish they had been there to see us. Silent Sam came to an inglorious end. A crowd of students tied him in ropes and pulled him off his pedestal. He was taken to an undisclosed location for his preservation. The remaining pedestal was removed and grass planted, and in a few weeks there would be no sign that he had ever been there.

The removal of Sam had repercussions throughout the state. The North Carolina legislature had mandated by law that Confederate memorials and statures could not be arbitrarily removed. The majority of citizens in North Carolina supported restoring Sam to his traditional place on the campus. The Chancellor of the university resigned under pressure.

The President of the university and the Board of Governors tried to affect a comprise and failed. Finally, Silent Sam was given to the Sons of the Confederate Veterans, along with a financial grant for his restoration. Silent Sam will not disappear from the south. Someday he will find a new home in a new location, and the question will continue; who is Silent Sam?

# Epilog

We seem to still face the conflict of Thomas Jefferson, the third president of the United States, and a complex and controversial founding father of our country. He wrote that all men are created equal and have the right to life, liberty, and the pursuit of happiness. Anyone should agree with that. He also wrote that the colored race was inherently inferior in mind and body to the white race, and their proper place was as slaves; he owned over six hundred slaves in his lifetime and only freed a few of them, several of whom he was their father.

With the current resurgence of the white supremacy movement in the United States, it seems this view is also still true for many people. At the University of North Carolina, the roles of enslaved African Americans who helped build the school are being examined to better understand their contribution and importance. The new Chancellor, Kevin Guskiewicz, has dedicated funds and human resources to this endeavor. It is a long-overdue continuation of the movement that began on Franklin Street in the 1960s.

The people of UNC; faculty and students and staff and athletic coaches and alumni think of themselves as part of the Carolina Family. It is a place for all people. Thomas Jefferson got it right when he founded the University of Virginia not as a house but a village; an Academical Village for all to learn together. Now places like this and like UNC are truly educational greens for all people; all men and women who are created equal. These places ensure that people in white robes and hoods, and attacks like Charlottesville will not succeed.

George and I were the lucky ones. We lived and studied for eight years at the greatest university in the country. We learned a lot from the teachers and our student friends and even from the outsiders who were active in the community in traditional or controversial ways. We also take pride in ourselves and believe that the university learned some things from us. Carolina is not the same place it was when George and I first enrolled there. The distance from Chapel Hill to Holly Springs and to Ahoskie is the same in miles but much closer in attitude and tolerance and understanding among all people. We think some of that started on Franklin Street, and we were there.

George and I are not finished yet. We will always be part of that greater Carolina Family. There are ball games to watch and Duke to beat; lectures and parties to attend and reunions to see who we can still remember. There are our scholarship students to visit with, to rejoin with the past ones, and to greet the new ones and be proud of all the things they will accomplish in their lives. There is Chapel Hill to visit and Suttons and the Coffee Shop where we can eat and the Carolina Inn and Ackland where George and I can again relive our memories and conversations.

The university campus is as beautiful as when the three-hundred-year-old Davie Poplar was first planted. The original buildings and the Old Well remain. We are at home here. George and Luke are old and black and white but are still united in the color of our priceless gem, Carolina Blue. We had a time. I wish you could have been there.

# BLACK WHITE AND CAROLINA BLUE

## DR. GEORGE T. GRIGSBY AND DR. LUCIUS BLANCHARD

Made in United States
Orlando, FL
13 August 2023